simply sweet ™

DECKED-OUT
DONUTS

simply sweet™

DECKED-OUT
DONUTS

125 OVER-THE-TOP TREATS
THAT TAKE
THE CAKE!

Oxmoor House®

TREAT YOURSELF!

Forget everything you know about donuts—complicated, labor-intensive, and just-for-breakfast—because you're about to discover a whole new world of exciting, brilliant, and easy donuts for the whole family! From Giant Strawberry Donuts (p. 49) and Lucky Shamrock Donuts (p. 64) to Piñata Donut Cakes (p. 114) and a Donut Beehive (p. 130), there's a recipe perfect for every party and occasion.

Sprinkled throughout, you'll find some interesting tidbits in our "Donut Trivia," and don't miss the helpful "Hot Tips" accompanying many of these recipes. If you're not up to starting from scratch but still want to make some amazing donut creations, check out the "Dolled-Up Donuts" chapter. Just look for the donut banner within every ingredient list, signaling whether you need homemade donuts or store-bought donuts—it's up to you!

Absolutely adorable, incredibly indulgent, and just plain fun, every single donut featured here is sure to impress your lucky guests. Dipped, swirled, glazed, and stuffed with dreamy flavors, these colorful creations take donuts to a whole new level.

Allison Cox Vasquez

EDITOR

CONTENTS

THE DONUT PANTRY

Get your kitchen ready with these essential ingredients, and you'll be set to make donuts anytime. The better your ingredients are, the better your donuts will turn out. Be picky!

- **FLOURS:** all-purpose flour or gluten-free flour

- **LEAVENERS:** active dry yeast, baking powder, and baking soda

- **FATS:** salted butter, peanut oil, and vegetable oil

- **COCOA POWDER:** regular cocoa powder and dark (Dutch process) cocoa powder

- **DAIRY:** whole milk, whole buttermilk, sour cream, cream cheese, and large eggs

- **SUGAR:** granulated white sugar, light brown sugar, and powdered sugar

- **EXTRAS:** multicolored sprinkles, nonpareils, colored sanding sugar, assorted candies, and chopped nuts

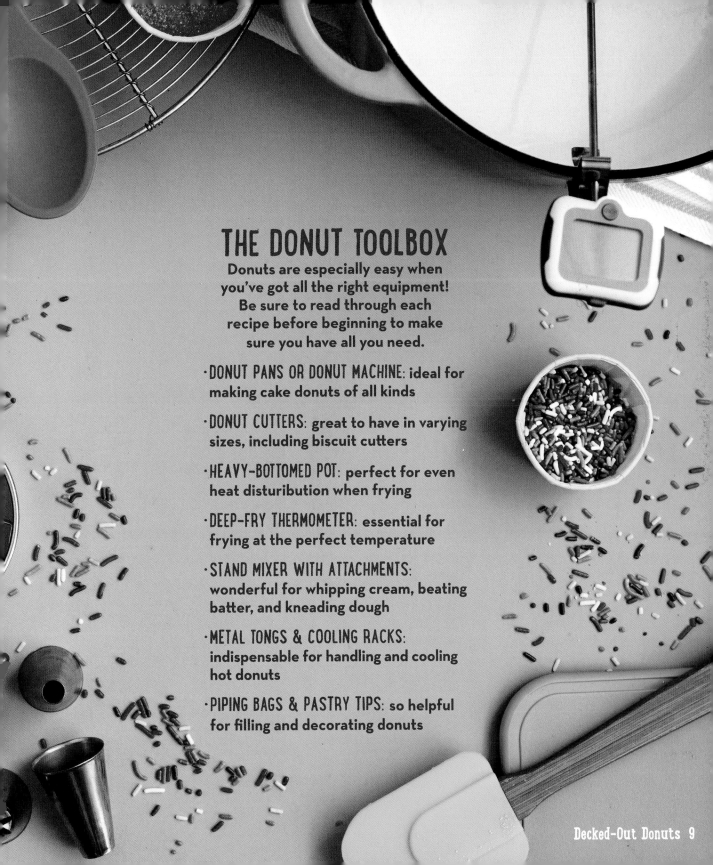

THE DONUT TOOLBOX

Donuts are especially easy when you've got all the right equipment! Be sure to read through each recipe before beginning to make sure you have all you need.

- **DONUT PANS OR DONUT MACHINE:** ideal for making cake donuts of all kinds

- **DONUT CUTTERS:** great to have in varying sizes, including biscuit cutters

- **HEAVY-BOTTOMED POT:** perfect for even heat disturibution when frying

- **DEEP-FRY THERMOMETER:** essential for frying at the perfect temperature

- **STAND MIXER WITH ATTACHMENTS:** wonderful for whipping cream, beating batter, and kneading dough

- **METAL TONGS & COOLING RACKS:** indispensable for handling and cooling hot donuts

- **PIPING BAGS & PASTRY TIPS:** so helpful for filling and decorating donuts

BASIC DONUTS
and glazes!

Learn how simple it is to make delicious donuts from scratch. Then top them off with a decadent icing or glaze!

FRIED CAKE DONUTS

**MAKES 12 DONUTS AND
12 DONUT HOLES
OR 48 DONUT HOLES
Hands-on 25 min.
Total 1 hour, 30 min.**

2 Tbsp. shortening,
   softened
1 cup granulated sugar
2 large eggs
4 cups sifted all-purpose
   flour
1 tsp. baking soda

1 tsp. table salt
$\frac{1}{4}$ tsp. ground cinnamon
$\frac{1}{8}$ tsp. ground nutmeg
1 cup buttermilk
Vegetable oil
Powdered sugar

1. Beat shortening at medium speed with an electric mixer until creamy; gradually add granulated sugar, beating well. Add eggs, 1 at a time, beating just until blended after each addition.

2. Combine flour and next 4 ingredients; add to shortening mixture alternately with buttermilk, beginning and ending with flour mixture. Beat at low speed just until blended after each addition. Cover and chill at least 1 hour.

3. Divide dough in half. Working with 1 portion at a time, place dough on a well-floured surface; roll to $\frac{1}{2}$-inch thickness. Cut into 12 donuts using a $3\frac{1}{2}$-inch floured donut cutter, re-rolling once, or cut out 48 donut holes using a $1\frac{1}{2}$-inch round cutter. Place cut donuts and donut holes on a floured baking sheet.

4. Pour oil to depth of $3\frac{1}{2}$ inches into a Dutch oven; heat to 375°. Fry donuts and donut holes, 4 of each at a time, 1 to $1\frac{1}{2}$ minutes on each side or until golden brown. Drain on a baking sheet lined with paper towels. Cool 5 minutes; dust with powdered sugar.

HOW TO FRY DONUTS

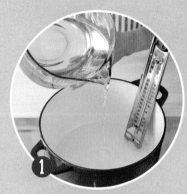

1 Pour oil to a depth of 3½ inches into a Dutch oven or a large heavy-bottomed pot. Heat to 375° using a candy thermometer.

2 Carefully place up to 4 donuts and 4 donut holes into heated oil, 1 at a time. Don't overcrowd them!

3 Each donut should cook for 1 to 1½ minutes on each side or until golden brown.

4 Drain donuts on a baking sheet lined with paper towels. Let cool 5 minutes.

5 Sprinkle donuts with powdered sugar or dip in desired glaze while they are still warm. If frosting, wait until donuts are completely cooled.

Dark cocoa and buttermilk make these home-style donuts all the more rich and indulgent. For a more decadent donut, dip in Vanilla Glaze (p. 32) or Classic Chocolate Glaze (p. 32).

CHOCOLATE CAKE DONUTS

**MAKES 12 DONUTS
AND 12 DONUT HOLES
OR 48 DONUT HOLES**
Hands-on 20 min.
Total 1 hour, 25 min.

2¾ cups all-purpose flour

1 cup unsweetened dark cocoa

2 tsp. baking powder

½ tsp. table salt

4 large eggs

1 cup granulated sugar

½ cup firmly packed light brown sugar

⅓ cup buttermilk

¼ cup butter, melted

½ tsp. vanilla extract

Vegetable oil

Powdered sugar

1. Whisk together first 4 ingredients in a large bowl. Whisk together eggs and next 5 ingredients; add to flour mixture, stirring just until moistened. Cover and chill 1 hour.

2. Pour oil to depth of 3½ inches into a large Dutch oven; heat to 375°. Turn dough out onto a well-floured surface, and roll to ½-inch thickness. Cut into 12 donuts using a 3½-inch floured donut cutter, re-rolling once, or cut out 48 donut holes using a 1½-inch round cutter. Place cut donuts and donut holes on a floured baking sheet.

3. Fry donuts and donut holes, 4 of each at a time, in hot oil 1 to 1½ minutes on each side or until done. Drain on paper towels. Cool 5 minutes; dust with powdered sugar.

BAKED DONUTS

MAKES 18 DONUTS
Hands-on 10 min.
Total 32 min.

No frying necessary here! Just stir together a quick-and-easy batter, pipe it into donut pans, and bake. Look for donut pans at craft stores or online. These donuts can also be glazed or simply dusted with powdered sugar.

Vegetable cooking spray

2 cups all-purpose flour

2 tsp. baking powder

1/4 tsp. table salt

1 3/4 cups sugar, divided

2 large eggs, lightly beaten

1 cup milk

1 tsp. vanilla extract

3/4 cup butter, melted and divided

1 Tbsp. ground cinnamon

1. Preheat oven to 400°. Lightly grease 2 (6-cavity) nonstick donut pans with cooking spray.

2. Whisk together flour, baking powder, salt, and 1 cup sugar in a large bowl. Make a well in center of mixture. Whisk together eggs, milk, vanilla, and 1/4 cup melted butter; add to flour mixture, stirring just until moistened.

3. Spoon batter into a large zip-top plastic freezer bag; seal bag. Snip a 3/4-inch hole in 1 corner of bag. Pipe batter into prepared donut pans, filling three-fourths full.

4. Bake at 400° for 9 minutes or until light golden. Cool in pans 2 minutes; transfer donuts to a wire rack. Repeat procedure with 1 donut pan, cooking spray, and remaining batter (wipe pan clean and allow to cool before re-using).

5. Combine cinnamon and remaining 3/4 cup sugar in a small bowl. Brush hot donuts with remaining 1/2 cup melted butter, and roll in sugar mixture.

HOT TIP

Piping the batter into the donut pans isn't required, but it sure makes it easier! You don't need a fancy piping bag—a plain zip-top plastic freezer bag will do the trick!

RAISED DONUTS

MAKES 24 DONUTS
AND 24 DONUT HOLES
OR 72 DONUT HOLES
Hands-on 30 min.
Total 1 hour, 20 min.

1 cup warm water (100°
    to 110°)
3 Tbsp. granulated sugar
1 (¼-oz.) envelope active
    dry yeast
⅓ cup shortening, melted
    and cooled
1 tsp. table salt
1 large egg
3 cups all-purpose flour
Parchment paper
Vegetable oil
1 cup powdered sugar

1. Combine first 3 ingredients in a large bowl; let stand 5 minutes.

2. Whisk in shortening, salt, and egg. Gradually stir in flour until a soft dough forms. Turn dough out onto a floured surface; knead 3 to 4 times.

3. Pat or roll dough to ¼-inch thickness. Cut into 24 donuts using a 3½-inch floured donut cutter, re-rolling once, or cut out 72 donut holes using a 1½-inch round cutter. Place cut donuts and donut holes on a baking sheet lined with parchment paper. Cover and let stand 45 minutes.

4. Pour oil to depth of 2 inches into a Dutch oven; heat to 375°. Fry donuts, in batches, 1 to 1½ minutes on each side or until golden. Drain on paper towels. Dust donuts with powdered sugar.

NOTE: To make donuts early in the morning for breakfast, dough may be chilled overnight. Cover and let donuts stand 1 hour before frying.

HOW TO MAKE RAISED DONUTS

1 Place warm water, sugar, and yeast in a large bowl, stirring to combine. Let stand for 5 minutes.

2 After whisking in shortening, salt, and egg, gradually add flour, stirring until a soft dough forms.

3 Turn dough out onto a floured surface, and knead 3 to 4 times.

4 Pat or roll dough to ¼-inch thickness, dusting with flour as needed.

5 Cut out donuts with a 3½-inch donut cutter.

6 Transfer donuts to a baking sheet lined with parchment paper, cover, and let rise for 45 minutes.

DONUT MACHINE DONUTS

MAKES 18 DONUTS
Hands-on 30 min.
Total 30 min.

Almost like a waffle iron, but with spaces for donut batter instead of waffle batter, a donut machine cooks up donuts quickly. Plus, they always turn out picture perfect!

1½ cups all-purpose flour	1 tsp. vanilla extract
½ cup sugar	1 large egg, lightly beaten
1½ tsp. baking powder	Cream Cheese Frosting
¼ tsp. table salt	(p. 35)
¾ cup buttermilk	Multicolored sprinkles or
½ cup butter, melted	colored sugars

1. Preheat a donut machine according to manufacturer's instructions. Whisk together first 4 ingredients in a medium bowl. Make a well in center of mixture. Combine buttermilk and next 3 ingredients; add to flour mixture, stirring just until moistened. Spoon batter into a large zip-top plastic freezer bag; seal bag. Snip a ¾-inch hole in 1 corner of bag. Pipe batter into cavities in donut machine, and bake according to manufacturer's instructions.

2. Carefully remove donuts from donut machine, and place on a wire rack. Repeat procedure with remaining batter. Let cool completely.

3. Prepare Cream Cheese Frosting. Frost donuts; sprinkle with sprinkles or colored sugars.

DONUT

In 1920, Adolph Levitt, a Russian refugee in New York City, invented the first donut machine.

TRIVIA

Just start with a can of refrigerated biscuits to make the easiest donuts ever. They fry up with a crispy exterior and light-as-air interior and taste like they're completely from scratch.

1 (7.5-oz.) can refrigerated buttermilk biscuits
Vegetable oil
1 cup sugar
1 Tbsp. ground cinnamon

1. Separate biscuits into individual rounds. Cut a hole in center of each biscuit with a ½-inch round cutter. Pour oil to depth of 2 inches into a Dutch oven; heat to 375°.

2. Fry donuts and donut holes, in batches, 30 seconds on each side or until golden. Drain on paper towels.

3. Combine sugar and cinnamon in a large zip-top plastic freezer bag. Add warm donuts and donut holes, a few at a time, to bag. Seal bag, and shake to coat.

SUPER-QUICK DONUTS

MAKES 10 DONUTS AND 10 DONUT HOLES OR 40 DONUT HOLES
Hands-on 15 min.
Total 15 min.

For a more intense cinnamon flavor, substitute a (12.4-oz.) can of refrigerated cinnamon rolls. Continue with recipe as directed. If desired, drizzle with cinnamon roll icing.

FLIP IT

EASY JELLY DONUTS

MAKES 24 DONUTS
Hands-on 30 min.
Total 1 hour, 45 min.

This decadent treat, made simple with frozen roll dough in place of homemade yeast dough, packs a sweet raspberry filling.

1 (25-oz.) package frozen bread roll dough, thawed according to package directions
Vegetable oil
½ cup granulated sugar
1¼ tsp. ground cinnamon
½ to 1 cup seedless raspberry jam*
Powdered sugar

1. Place rolls 2 inches apart on 2 lightly greased baking sheets. Cover and let rise in a warm place (85°), free from drafts, according to package directions.

2. Pour oil to a depth of 2 inches into a Dutch oven; heat to 350°. Fry rolls, in batches, 1 to 1½ minutes on each side or until fully cooked and golden brown. Drain on a wire rack over paper towels.

3. Whisk together granulated sugar and cinnamon in a medium bowl. Add warm donuts to sugar mixture, tossing to coat. Let cool completely on wire rack (about 15 minutes).

4. Make a small slit in side of each donut, using a paring knife. Place jam in a zip-top plastic freezer bag (do not seal). Snip 1 corner of bag to make a small hole. Pipe jam into each donut. Dust with powdered sugar.

*Strawberry jelly may be substituted.

NOTE: We tested with Bridgford Proof & Bake Parkerhouse White Yeast Rolls frozen bread dough.

These old-fashioned donuts evoke delicious memories of childhood with their crispy ridges that help capture the glaze.

5 cups cake flour

4 tsp. baking powder

2 tsp. table salt

1 cup sugar

1/4 cup shortening

4 egg yolks

1 1/2 cups sour cream

Vegetable oil

Vanilla Glaze (p. 32)

OLD-FASHIONED DONUTS

**MAKES 12 DONUTS
AND 12 DONUT HOLES
OR 48 DONUT HOLES**
Hands-on 39 min.
Total 1 hour, 39 min.

1. Whisk together first 3 ingredients in a medium bowl. Beat sugar and shortening at medium speed with a heavy-duty electric stand mixer 1 minute or until mixture resembles wet sand. Add egg yolks, 1 at a time, beating just until blended after each addition. Beat 1 minute on medium speed or until mixture is pale in color.

2. Add flour mixture to shortening mixture alternately with sour cream, beginning and ending with flour mixture. Beat at low speed just until blended after each addition, stopping to scrape bowl as needed. (Dough will be sticky.) Transfer dough to a clean bowl. Cover and refrigerate at least 1 hour (up to 24 hours).

3. Roll out dough on a heavily floured surface to 1/2-inch thickness. Cut dough with a 3 1/4-inch floured donut cutter.

4. Pour oil to depth of 3 1/2 inches into a Dutch oven; heat to 350°. Drop donuts and donut holes, 3 of each at a time, into hot oil. Fry 20 seconds; gently turn over, and cook 1 minute or until golden brown and cracked. Turn again, and cook first side for 1 minute or until golden brown. Drain on paper towels. Dip 1 side of warm donuts in Vanilla Glaze.

FRENCH CRULLERS

MAKES 10 DONUTS
Hands-on 38 min.
Total 1 hour, 28 min.

Parchment paper
½ cup unsalted butter,
    cut into 8 pieces
2 tsp. sugar
½ tsp. table salt
1 cup all-purpose flour
4 large eggs
Vegetable oil
Vanilla Glaze (p. 32)

1. Cover a large baking sheet with parchment paper. Draw 10 (2½-inch) circles on parchment paper. Turn parchment paper over; secure with masking tape.

2. Combine 1 cup water, butter, and next 2 ingredients in a heavy saucepan. Bring to a boil over medium-high heat. Quickly stir in flour all at once. Beat with a wooden spoon 1 minute or until mixture is smooth and leaves sides of pan, forming a ball of dough. Cook, stirring constantly, 2 minutes. Transfer mixture to the bowl of a heavy-duty electric stand mixer fitted with paddle attachment. Cool mixture 5 minutes.

3. Beating at medium speed, add 3 eggs, 1 at a time, to batter, stopping to scrape bowl after each addition. Gradually add enough of 1 beaten egg, 1 Tbsp. at a time, beating until dough is smooth and glossy.

4. Spoon dough into a pastry bag fitted with a ½-inch closed star tip. Pipe dough onto prepared baking sheet, outlining circles drawn on parchment paper. Freeze 45 minutes or until very firm.

5. Pour oil to depth of 3 inches into Dutch oven; heat to 375°. Fry donuts, 3 or 4 at a time, 2½ to 3 minutes on each side or until golden brown. Drain on paper towels. Cool completely. Dip donuts in Vanilla Glaze.

NOTE: For ease in drawing circles on parchment paper, trace around a 2½-inch biscuit cutter or juice glass.

HOW TO MAKE FRENCH CRULLERS

1 Combine water, butter, sugar, and salt in a heavy saucepan. Bring to a boil over medium-high heat. Dump in all the flour at once.

2 Beat vigorously with a wooden spoon for 1 minute or until mixture is smooth and leaves sides of pan, forming a ball of dough.

3 Cook dough, stirring constantly, for 2 minutes more. Transfer mixture to the bowl of a heavy-duty electric stand mixer fitted with paddle attachment. Cool mixture 5 minutes.

4 Beating at medium speed, add 3 eggs, 1 at a time, to batter, stopping to scrape bowl after each addition.

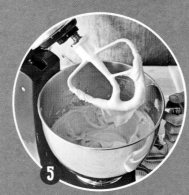

5 Gradually add enough of 1 beaten egg, 1 Tbsp. at a time, beating until dough is smooth and glossy.

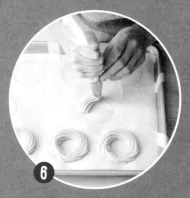

6 Spoon dough into a pastry bag fitted with a ½-inch closed star tip. Pipe dough onto prepared baking sheet, outlining circles drawn on parchment paper. Freeze 45 minutes or until very firm.

By using gluten-free baking mix for these donuts, you can avoid any specialty flours and thickener that you would normally need for a gluten-free baked good. Baking powder and baking soda make these donuts airy and light, but the added yeast gives them great donut flavor!

GLUTEN-FREE DONUTS

MAKES 12 DONUTS
Hands-on 7 min.
Total 1 hour, 9 min.

2 cups gluten-free biscuit
    and baking mix

¾ cup sugar

1½ tsp. baking powder

½ tsp. table salt

⅛ tsp. baking soda

1 (¼-oz.) envelope
    rapid-rise yeast

½ cup warm water
    (120° to 130°)

½ cup butter, melted

1 tsp. vanilla extract

1 large egg

Vegetable cooking spray

1. Combine first 6 ingredients in a large bowl; make a well in center of mixture. Whisk together warm water and next 3 ingredients; add to dry mixture, stirring just until moistened. Cover and let stand 10 minutes.

2. Preheat oven to 350°. Lightly grease 2 (6-cavity) nonstick donut pans with cooking spray. Place batter in a large zip-top plastic freezer bag. Snip 1 corner of bag to make a ¾-inch hole. Fill each cavity three-fourths full.

3. Bake at 350° for 12 minutes or until golden brown. Cool in pans on wire racks 10 minutes. Remove from pans to wire racks, and cool completely (about 30 minutes).

HOT TIP

If you don't have 2 (6-cavity) donut pans, bake donuts in 2 batches, allowing pan to cool and wiping out with a paper towel before re-filling.

VANILLA GLAZE

MAKES ABOUT 1 CUP
Hands-on 3 min.
Total 3 min.

This is a translucent glaze perfect for drizzling or dipping. Use clear vanilla extract, or omit the vanilla for a perfectly white glaze. For a colored version, add a drop at a time of food coloring to finished glaze until you get the shade you want.

2 cups powdered sugar   4 to 5 Tbsp. milk
½ tsp. vanilla extract

1. Whisk together powdered sugar, vanilla, and 4 Tbsp. milk. Add 1 Tbsp. milk, if needed, to reach desired consistency.

CLASSIC CHOCOLATE GLAZE

MAKES 1 CUP
Hands-on 5 min.
Total 5 min.

Rich and chocolatey, this glaze is thin enough to dip donuts directly into it for that classic donut-shop look. Or you can drizzle it over just about any cooled donut.

¼ cup half-and-half   ½ cup powdered sugar
1 cup semisweet chocolate
    morsels

1. Microwave half-and-half in a microwave-safe bowl at HIGH 1 minute or until hot. Add chocolate morsels, stirring until smooth. Stir in powdered sugar. Use immediately.

THICK VANILLA ICING

This opaque icing can coat both donuts and donut holes. Omit the vanilla extract, or use clear extract for a perfectly white icing. Add food coloring to achieve any color.

6 cups powdered sugar

1 tsp. vanilla extract

½ cup plus 1 to 2 Tbsp. milk

1. Whisk together powdered sugar, vanilla, and ½ cup milk until creamy. Add 1 to 2 Tbsp. additional milk, whisking until very thick but still pourable.

Strawberry Icing Variation: Make a Fresh Strawberry Icing by reducing milk to 2 Tbsp., omitting vanilla, and adding ¾ cup pureed fresh strawberries. Adjust consistency with more powdered sugar or milk as needed.

MAKES 2½ CUPS
Hands-on 3 min.
Total 3 min.

CREAM CHEESE FROSTING

Ideal as a flavorful, velvety coating on any substantial donut, this frosting lends itself well to colors. You can tint it any shade with food coloring; just add a couple drops at a time to reach the desired shade.

1 (8-oz.) package cream cheese, softened

½ cup butter, softened

3 cups powdered sugar

1 tsp. vanilla extract

1. Beat cream cheese and butter at medium speed with an electric mixer until creamy. Gradually add powdered sugar and vanilla, beating at low speed until blended. Increase speed to medium, and beat until fluffy.

Peanut Butter Frosting Variation: Make a Peanut Butter Frosting by substituting ½ cup creamy peanut butter for butter. Continue with recipe as directed.

MAKES 2½ CUPS
Hands-on 5 min.
Total 5 min.

DOLLED-UP DONUTS

Discover a world of the happiest donuts ever,
where wondrous themes and adorable faces abound,
and superfun flavors and designs make the
whole family say, "Wow!"

MIX & MATCH DONUTS

 +  +

START
BASIC DONUT

1. RAISED DONUTS (P. 18)
2. OLD-FASHIONED DONUTS (P. 27)
3. CHOCOLATE CAKE DONUTS (P. 15)

ADD
GLAZE

1. CLASSIC CHOCOLATE GLAZE (P. 32)
2. CREAM CHEESE FROSTING (P. 35)
3. STRAWBERRY ICING (P. 35)
4. PEANUT BUTTER FROSTING (P. 35)

FINISH
TOPPINGS!

1. TOASTED COCONUT
2. CHOPPED TOASTED NUTS
3. FRESH BERRIES
4. MULTICOLORED SPRINKLES
5. ASSORTED CANDIES

= 60 DELICIOUS COMBINATIONS

Create your own donut match-ups,
or try one of our genius combinations. →

FRESH STRAWBERRY DONUTS
RAISED DONUTS +
STRAWBERRY ICING +
SLICED STRAWBERRIES

TRIPLE CHOCOLATE DONUTS
CHOCOLATE CAKE DONUTS +
CLASSIC CHOCOLATE GLAZE + MINI
CANDY-COATED CHOCOLATE PIECES

PEANUT BUTTER CUP DONUTS
CHOCOLATE CAKE DONUTS +
PEANUT BUTTER FROSTING +
CHOPPED ROASTED PEANUTS

ITALIAN CREAM CAKE DONUTS
RAISED DONUTS +
CREAM CHEESE FROSTING +
CHOPPED TOASTED PECANS

BIRTHDAY CAKE DONUTS
OLD-FASHIONED DONUTS +
CLASSIC CHOCOLATE GLAZE +
MULTICOLORED SPRINKLES

FRUITY RAINBOW DONUTS
OLD-FASHIONED DONUTS +
STRAWBERRY ICING + RAINBOW-
COLORED FRUIT-FLAVORED
CANDIES

PEANUT BUTTER & BERRY DONUTS
RAISED DONUTS +
PEANUT BUTTER FROSTING +
FRESH BLACKBERRIES
AND RASPBERRIES

STRAWBERRY-COVERED CHOCOLATE DONUTS
CHOCOLATE CAKE DONUTS +
STRAWBERRY ICING +
CHOPPED STRAWBERRIES

COCONUT CREAM DONUTS
OLD-FASHIONED DONUTS +
CREAM CHEESE FROSTING +
TOASTED COCONUT

These adorable, hot-pink piglet faces will have everyone squealing with delight!

Fried Cake Donuts (pg. 12) or 12 store-bought cake donuts and 8 donut holes

Thick Vanilla Icing
    (p. 35)
Electric pink food
    coloring paste
Deep pink food
    coloring paste

Parchment or wax paper
1 (0.67-oz.) tube black
    decorating gel
1 (7-oz.) pouch white
    cookie icing

PIGGY DONUTS

MAKES 8 DONUTS
Hands-on 1 hour, 15 min.
Total 2 hours, 45 min.

1. Prepare Cake Donuts. Cool completely. (Do not dust with powdered sugar.) Prepare Thick Vanilla Icing. Transfer ¾ cup icing to a separate bowl; tint with desired amount of electric pink food coloring paste. Tint remaining 1¾ cups icing with desired amount of deep pink food coloring paste.

2. Dip 8 donuts into deep pink icing, letting excess drip back into bowl. Place on a wire rack set over a baking sheet lined with parchment or wax paper. Dip each of 8 donut holes in electric pink icing, and place in center of each donut. Reserve remaining 4 donut holes for another use.

3. Cut remaining 4 donuts into quarters. Dip donut quarters into deep pink icing; attach to donuts, 1 on each side, to resemble ears. Let stand 30 minutes or until icing is set.

4. Working with 1 donut at a time, pipe 2 dots of black decorating gel on each donut, above donut holes, to resemble eyes. Pipe 2 dots of white cookie icing in center of donut hole "snout" to resemble nostrils. Let stand 30 minutes or until icing and decorations are set.

NOTE: We tested with Betty Crocker Decorating Cookie Icing.

HIPPY DIPPY DONUTS

MAKES 24 DONUTS
Hands-on 1 hour, 15 min.
Total 2 hours, 45 min.

HOT TIP

Be sure to complete the icing and decorating of donuts one at a time so that the icing stays wet and workable as you create your design.

Fried Cake Donuts (p. 12)

1 (6-inch) wooden skewer
2 cups marshmallow
    crème
Thick Vanilla Icing (p. 35)

Pink food coloring paste
Yellow food coloring paste
Green food coloring paste

1. Prepare Fried Cake Donuts, rolling chilled dough to ¼-inch thickness and cutting out donuts with a 3-inch round biscuit cutter. Cool completely. (Do not dust with powdered sugar.)

2. Make a small hole in the side of each donut using a 6-inch wooden skewer. Insert plain metal tip no. 5 into a large decorating bag; fill with marshmallow crème. Insert tip into holes; squirt crème into centers of donuts.

3. Prepare Thick Vanilla Icing. Tint ⅓ cup icing with desired amount of pink food coloring paste, ⅓ cup icing with desired amount of yellow food coloring paste, and ⅓ cup icing with desired amount of green food coloring paste. Do not tint remaining 1½ cups icing. Spoon each color of tinted icing into a separate 1-qt. zip-top plastic freezer bag. Snip 1 corner of each bag to make a small hole.

4. Working with 1 donut at a time, spread white icing over surface of donut. Immediately squeeze colored icings in stripes, dots, or spiral patterns on top of iced donut, and drag a wooden pick through colored icings to create different designs.

Rise and shine to clever donuts that only look like a fried egg! Pair these sweet treats with crisp bacon and a side of fresh fruit to round out a tasty breakfast.

Raised Donuts (p. 18)

1 (6-inch) wooden skewer
1½ cups jarred lemon curd
½ recipe Thick Vanilla
    Icing (p. 35)

3 drops yellow liquid food
    coloring
Garnish: grated chocolate

1. Prepare Raised Donuts, cutting out donuts with a 2½-inch round biscuit cutter. Cool completely. (Do not dust with powdered sugar.)

2. Make a small hole in the side of each donut using a 6-inch wooden skewer. Insert plain metal tip no. 5 into a large decorating bag; fill with lemon curd. Insert tip into holes; squirt curd into centers of donuts.

3. Prepare ½ recipe Thick Vanilla Icing. Transfer 5 Tbsp. icing to a small bowl. Add food coloring, stirring until blended.

4. Spread white icing evenly over tops of donuts. Let stand until set. Spoon ¼ tsp. yellow icing in center of each donut to resemble an egg yolk. Let stand until set.

SUNNY-SIDE-UP DONUTS

MAKES 24 DONUTS
Hands-on 1 hour, 15 min.
Total 2 hours, 30 min.

DONUT

Have you ever dunked your donut in your coffee? Apparently, actress Mae Murray was the first to do so: she dropped her donut into her coffee by accident while filming at Lindy's Deli in New York City, and the trend stuck!

TRIVIA

FRUITY CEREAL DONUTS

MAKES 12 DONUTS • HANDS-ON 36 MIN. • TOTAL 1 HOUR, 56 MIN.

2 Tbsp. shortening

1 cup granulated sugar

2 large eggs

4½ cups all-purpose flour

1 tsp. baking soda

1 tsp. table salt

1 cup buttermilk

1 cup fruit-flavored crisp rice
   cereal, divided

Vegetable oil

Thick Vanilla Icing (p. 35)

1. Beat shortening at medium speed with an electric mixer until creamy; gradually add granulated sugar, beating well. Add eggs, 1 at a time, beating just until blended after each addition.

2. Combine flour, baking soda, and salt; add to shortening mixture alternately with buttermilk, beginning and ending with flour mixture. Beat at low speed just until blended after each addition, stopping to scrape bowl as needed. Stir in ½ cup cereal. Cover and chill 1 hour.

3. Pour oil to depth of 3 inches in a Dutch oven; heat to 375°.

4. Divide dough in half. Working with 1 portion at a time, place dough on a heavily-floured surface; roll to ¼-inch thickness. Cut dough with a floured 4-inch donut cutter.

5. Fry donuts, 3 to 4 at a time, 1 minute on each side. Drain on paper towels. Cool completely.

6. Prepare Thick Vanilla Icing in a medium bowl. Dip tops of donuts in icing. Sprinkle with remaining ½ cup cereal.

NOTE: We tested with Post Fruity Pebbles.

- Substitute apple-flavored O-shaped cereal for fruity cereal (chop cereal for dough).
- Sprinkle donuts with O-shaped cereal and chopped dried apple chips.

APPLE-A-DAY DONUTS

PEANUT-BUTTER CEREAL DONUTS

- Substitute peanut butter and chocolate-flavored corn cereal for fruity cereal.
- Add 1 Tbsp. creamy peanut butter to Thick Vanilla Icing.

CHOCOLATE CEREAL DONUTS

- Substitute chocolate-flavored puffed rice cereal for fruity cereal.
- Omit Thick Vanilla Icing.
- Dip donuts in 1 (16-oz.) container melted dark chocolate frosting.

Filled with luscious strawberry jam and topped with a sprinkling of chocolate "seeds," these springtime-inspired donuts are both festive and delicious.

GIANT STRAWBERRY DONUTS

MAKES 20 DONUTS
Hands-on 1 hour, 15 min.
Total 2 hours, 30 min.

Raised Donuts (p. 18)

1 (6-inch) wooden skewer
1¼ cups seedless strawberry jam
½ recipe Thick Vanilla Icing (p. 35)
Red food coloring paste
Green food coloring paste
¼ cup mini-morsels

1. Prepare Raised Donuts, cutting dough with a 3½-inch strawberry-shaped cookie cutter. Cool completely. (Do not dust with powdered sugar.)

2. Make a small hole in the side of each donut using a 6-inch wooden skewer. Insert plain metal tip no. 5 into a large decorating bag; fill with strawberry jam. Insert tip into holes; squirt jam into centers of donuts.

3. Prepare Thick Vanilla Icing. Tint 1 cup icing with desired amount of red food coloring paste. Tint remaining ¼ cup icing with desired amount of green food coloring paste.

4. Working with 1 donut at a time, spread red icing over surface of donut. Immediately sprinkle donut with mini-morsels to resemble seeds.

5. Insert plain metal tip no. 5 into a decorating bag; fill with green icing. Pipe green icing onto donuts to resemble leaves.

MAPLE-BACON PUPPY-DOG DONUTS

MAKES 24 DONUTS
Hands-on 1 hour, 15 min.
Total 2 hours, 45 min.

HOT TIP

Feel free to decorate your donut puppies as you please. Use small cookies for ears and any candies for the face. You can even turn them into donut kitties!

Your family will beg for one of these adorably delicious treats, which combine two of our favorite flavors: bacon and maple syrup!

Fried Cake Donuts (p. 12)

¾ cup cooked and finely chopped bacon slices (12 slices)
Thick Vanilla Icing (p. 35)
2 Tbsp. maple syrup
½ tsp. pure maple extract
16 cooked bacon slices, each broken into thirds

72 large and small brown candy-coated milk chocolate pieces
1 (0.67-oz.) tube black decorating gel

1. Prepare Fried Cake Donuts, adding ¾ cup crumbled bacon to dough, rolling chilled dough to ¼-inch thickness, and cutting out donuts with a 3-inch round biscuit cutter. Cool completely. (Do not dust with powdered sugar.)

2. Prepare Thick Vanilla Icing. Stir maple syrup and pure maple extract into icing.

3. Working with 1 donut at a time, dip top half of donut in maple icing, and place, iced side up, on a wire rack. Gently adhere 2 bacon pieces onto donut for ears, 2 candy-coated chocolate pieces for eyes, and 1 candy-coated chocolate piece in center of donut for nose. Using decorating gel, pipe arcs for mouth.

NOTE: We tested with M&M's.

These fun donuts, with fresh carrots, are a perfect springtime or Easter treat. Pair them with Fuzzy Chickadee Donut Holes on p. 89 for a sweet duo.

Fried Cake Donuts (p. 12)

²/₃ cup finely chopped pecans, toasted

1 cup finely shredded carrot (about 3 medium)

Vegetable oil

Cream Cheese Frosting (p. 35)

⅛ tsp. green food coloring paste

⅛ tsp. orange food coloring paste

Garnish: colored sanding sugars

1. Prepare Fried Cake Donuts through Step 2, folding in pecans and carrot after last addition of flour mixture.

2. Divide dough in half. Working with 1 portion at a time, place dough on a heavily floured surface; roll to ½-inch thickness. Cut out donuts with a 4-inch floured carrot-shaped cutter.

3. Pour oil to depth of 3½ inches in a Dutch oven; heat to 375°. Fry donuts, 4 at a time, 1 to 1½ minutes on each side or until golden brown. Drain on paper towels. Cool completely.

4. Prepare Cream Cheese Frosting. Transfer ¾ cup frosting to a small bowl, and stir in green food coloring paste.

5. Add orange food coloring paste to remaining 1¾ cups frosting. Spoon each color frosting into a separate 1-qt. zip-top plastic freezer bag (do not seal). Snip 1 corner of each bag to make a small hole. Pipe orange frosting onto carrot, and green frosting onto carrot top.

CARROT CAKE DONUTS

MAKES 24 DONUTS
Hands-on 1 hour, 15 min.
Total 2 hours, 45 min.

WISE OLD OWL DONUTS

MAKES 24 DONUTS
Hands-on 1 hour, 15 min.
Total 2 hours, 30 min.

These colorful and festive owl treats will brighten up any birthday celebration or children's buffet.

Raised Donuts (p. 18) or 24 store-bought yeast donuts

Classic Chocolate Glaze (p. 32)

Parchment or wax paper

48 large candy eyes

24 candy corn candies

96 orange jelly beans (about 1½ cups)

1 cup sliced almonds

1. Prepare Raised Donuts. Cool completely. (Do not dust with powdered sugar.) Cool donut holes 5 minutes; dust with powdered sugar, and reserve for another use.

2. Prepare Classic Chocolate Glaze. Dip donuts in glaze, allowing excess to drip back into the bowl. Place glazed donuts on a rack set over a baking sheet lined with parchment or wax paper.

3. While glaze is soft, gently press 2 candy eyes close together at top of each donut. Gently press 1 candy corn between eyes, with tip pointing downward, to resemble a beak. Press 4 jelly beans in bottom center of each donut to resemble feet.

4. Press 7 to 8 almond slices in 4 overlapping rows along both sides of each donut to resemble wings.

Children and garden enthusiasts alike are sure to adore these brightly colored, flower-shaped whimsical treats!

SPRING FLING DONUTS

MAKES 24 DONUTS
Hands-on 1 hour, 15 min.
Total 2 hours, 30 min.

Raised Donuts (p. 18)

Cream Cheese Frosting (p. 35)

Food coloring paste, in desired color

2 Tbsp. sprinkles, in desired color

6 (.55-oz.) packages green apple-flavored taffy candy (optional)

24 green wooden craft sticks (optional)

1. Prepare Raised Donuts, cutting out donuts with a 3-inch flower-shaped cookie cutter. Cool completely. (Do not dust with powdered sugar.)

2. Prepare Cream Cheese Frosting. Tint frosting with desired amount of food coloring paste.

3. Frost donuts with frosting; sprinkle centers with desired color of sprinkles. Repeat procedure with remaining donuts, frosting, and desired color of sprinkles.

4. If desired, cut out leaf shapes from candy; press firmly onto craft sticks, and insert into bottoms of donuts to resemble flower stems.

NOTE: We tested with Airheads green apple–flavored taffy candies.

HOT TIP

Serve these donuts at your next garden party or spring fling! Arrange donut flowers in cups or glasses filled with candies or sprinkles.

PB&J DONUTS

MAKES 16 DONUTS
Hands-on 45 min.
Total 3 hours

A hint of peanut butter in the dough makes a play on the iconic childhood favorite.

½ cup milk
½ cup creamy peanut butter
1 (¼-oz.) envelope active dry yeast
¼ cup warm water (100° to 110°)
1 large egg, lightly beaten
2¾ cups all-purpose flour
¼ cup granulated sugar
½ tsp. kosher salt
Parchment paper
Vegetable oil
1 cup strawberry jelly
1 cup sifted powdered sugar

1. Combine milk and peanut butter in a small saucepan. Cook, stirring constantly, over low heat until smooth. Remove from heat. Let cool.

2. Combine yeast and warm water in bowl of a heavy-duty electric stand mixer; let stand 5 minutes. Add peanut butter mixture and egg. Add flour, granulated sugar, and salt to bowl; beat at low speed, using dough hook attachment, 4 to 5 minutes or until dough begins to leave the sides of the bowl, pulls together, and becomes soft and smooth. Place in a well-greased bowl, turning to grease top. Cover and let rise in a warm place (85°), free from drafts, 1 hour or until doubled in bulk.

3. Turn dough out onto a floured surface, and roll into a 10- x 8-inch rectangle. Cut dough into 16 (2½ x 2-inch) rectangles. Transfer to a baking sheet lined with parchment paper. Cover and let rise until doubled in bulk (about 1 hour).

4. Pour oil to depth of 2 inches into a Dutch oven; heat to 350°. Fry donuts, 4 at a time, 1 minute on each side. Drain on paper towels. Cool 5 minutes. Cut each donut in half horizontally. Spread 1 Tbsp. jelly on bottom halves of donuts; cover with donut tops. Cut each donut sandwich in half diagonally. Dust with powdered sugar.

Use the bottom of a piping tip as a ¾-inch cutter, or look for small fondant cutters to cut out the mini donut centers.

1 (15.25-oz.) package
    yellow cake mix
½ cup buttermilk
2 Tbsp. unsalted butter,
    melted
3 large eggs
1½ cups cake flour
½ tsp. ground cinnamon

Vegetable oil
Thick Vanilla Icing (p. 35)
Dash pink food coloring gel
½ cup multicolored
    sprinkles
46 mini colored drinking
    straws or lollipop sticks

1. Beat cake mix, buttermilk, melted butter, eggs, cake flour, and cinnamon by hand with a wooden spoon until blended. Chill dough until firm (about 1 hour).

2. Place dough on a lightly floured surface, and roll to ½-inch thickness. Cut with a 1½-inch round cutter, flouring the cutter frequently. Cut a circle out of center of each doughnut with a ¾-inch round cutter.

3. Pour oil to depth of 2 inches into a Dutch oven; heat over medium heat to 365°. Fry doughnuts, in batches, about 30 seconds on each side or until golden brown. Drain on paper towels, and cool completely before glazing.

4. Prepare Thick Vanilla Icing. Stir pink food coloring gel into icing until well blended. Dip 1 side of each doughnut in icing; top with sprinkles. Insert a straw or lollipop stick into 1 end of each donut. Let stand 30 minutes or until icing is set.

MINI GLAZED DONUT POPS

MAKES 46 POPS
Hands-on 25 min.
Total 2 hours, 15 min.

DONUT

National Donut Day is always the first Friday in June, so mark your calendar and throw a donut party to celebrate!

TRIVIA

BOSTON CREAM HEARTS

MAKES 24 DONUTS • HANDS-ON 1 HOUR, 15 MIN. • TOTAL 2 HOURS, 30 MIN.

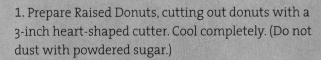

Raised Donuts (p. 18)

¼ cup sugar

2 Tbsp. cornstarch

¼ tsp. table salt

2 cups milk

2 large egg yolks

1 tsp. vanilla extract

Classic Chocolate Glaze (p. 32)

½ recipe Thick Vanilla Icing
   (p. 35)

1. Prepare Raised Donuts, cutting out donuts with a 3-inch heart-shaped cutter. Cool completely. (Do not dust with powdered sugar.)

2. Whisk together sugar and next 4 ingredients in a heavy saucepan. Bring to a boil over medium heat, whisking constantly. Boil, whisking constantly, 1 to 1½ minutes or until thickened. Remove pan from heat. Stir in vanilla.

3. Fill a large bowl with ice. Place pan containing milk mixture in ice, and let stand, stirring occasionally, 20 minutes. Place plastic wrap directly onto custard (to prevent a film from forming), and chill thoroughly.

4. Insert a round metal tip no. 5 into a large decorating bag; fill with custard. Insert tip into side of each donut, and fill with custard.

5. Prepare Classic Chocolate Glaze and Thick Vanilla Icing.

6. Dip donuts into Chocolate Glaze. Spoon Thick Vanilla Icing into a 1-qt. zip-top plastic freezer bag. Snip 1 corner of bag to make a small hole. Squirt a zigzag drizzle over donuts.

CHOCOLATE COOKIE HEARTS

- Omit Classic Chocolate Glaze.
- Stir ½ cup chocolate chips into hot cooked custard.
- Prepare full recipe Thick Vanilla Icing, and frost all donuts with it.
- Sprinkle crushed cream-filled chocolate sandwich cookies onto donuts.

CHRISTMAS TREE BOSTON CREAMS

- Cut dough into tree shapes.
- Omit Classic Chocolate Glaze.
- Prepare full recipe Thick Vanilla Icing; tint icing green and frost donuts.
- Sprinkle white and red candies onto frosted donuts.

LEMON CREAM HEARTS

- Omit vanilla extract and Classic Chocolate Glaze.
- Add 2 tsp. lemon zest to hot custard.
- Prepare full recipe Thick Vanilla Icing; reserve ¼ cup, and set aside.
- Tint remaining icing yellow, and frost donuts; drizzle with white icing.

LUCKY SHAMROCK DONUTS

MAKES 14 DONUTS
Hands-on 45 min.
Total 2 hours, 15 min.

These donuts are a chocolate lover's dream. Plus, they are packed with lots of luck!

Chocolate Cake Donuts (p. 15)

½ recipe Thick Vanilla Icing (p. 35)

Leaf green food coloring paste

¾ cup green and light green sprinkles

1. Prepare Chocolate Cake Donuts, cutting dough with a 3½-inch shamrock-shaped cutter. Cool completely. (Do not dust with powdered sugar.)

2. Prepare Thick Vanilla Icing; tint icing with desired amount of leaf green food coloring paste. Spread icing over tops of donuts; sprinkle with sprinkles.

DONUT

Every year, more than 10 billion donuts are produced in the United States. That's more than 30 donuts per person per year!

TRIVIA

All eyes are on our spooky monster donuts—the perfect treat for your next ghoulish get-together!

Chocolate Cake Donuts (p. 15) or 12 store-bought chocolate cake donuts

½ recipe Thick Vanilla Icing (p. 35)

Neon green food coloring paste

1 (0.67-oz.) tube black decorating gel

Assorted small candy eyes

1. Prepare Chocolate Cake Donuts. Cool completely. (Do not dust with powdered sugar.)

2. Prepare ½ recipe Thick Vanilla Icing; tint with desired amount of green food coloring paste.

3. Spoon icing over donuts. Draw a mouth on each donut using black decorating gel. Sprinkle each donut with desired number of candy eyes.

GREEN & MEAN MONSTER DONUTS

MAKES 12 DONUTS
Hands-on 45 min.
Total 2 hours, 15 min.

HOT TIP

What color are your monsters? Ours are bright green, but if yours are blue, pink, or purple, it's easy to change the icing color!

CANDY CANE DONUTS

MAKES 16 DONUTS
Hands-on 45 min.
Total 2 hours, 15 min.

The chocolate-peppermint flavor combination in this donut tastes like a peppermint patty, but if you prefer classic pure peppermint flavor, substitute the Raised Donuts (p. 18) for the Chocolate Cake Donuts.

FLIP IT

These decadent donuts will be a hit at your next holiday gathering. Simply omit the peppermint extract if you want a traditional chocolate flavor.

Chocolate Cake Donuts (p. 15)

$3/4$ tsp. peppermint extract, divided

Thick Vanilla Icing (p. 35)

White candy sprinkles

Red candy sprinkles

1. Prepare Chocolate Cake Donuts, using $1/2$ tsp. peppermint extract instead of vanilla extract and cutting with a 4-inch candy cane-shaped cutter. Cool completely. (Do not dust with powdered sugar.)

2. Prepare Thick Vanilla Icing, stirring in remaining $1/4$ tsp. peppermint extract. Spread donuts with icing. Sprinkle donuts with white and red candy sprinkles in alternating bands to resemble candy canes.

HOLEY DONUTS!

Oh-so-cute and extra-clever, these tiny
treats are easy to decorate and perfect for sharing.
Start with homemade donut holes,
or buy them from the store and get glazing!

DONUT
FONDUE PARTY

Gather all the elements below, plus mini forks, picks, sticks, or sturdy straws to get dipping and topping!

 +  +

MAKE
DONUTS

1. RAISED DONUT HOLES (MAKE OR BUY) (P. 18)

2. CHOCOLATE CAKE DONUT HOLES (MAKE OR BUY) (P. 15)

DIP
FONDUE

1. 2 (16-OZ.) CONTAINERS FRENCH VANILLA FROSTING, MELTED

2. 2 (16-OZ.) CONTAINERS DARK CHOCOLATE FROSTING, MELTED

3. 2 (16-OZ.) CONTAINERS STRAWBERRY FROSTING, MELTED

SPRINKLE
TOPPINGS

1. MULTICOLORED SPRINKLES

2. MINI-MORSELS

3. CHOPPED TOASTED NUTS

4. COLORFUL CEREALS

5. MINI CANDIES & CHOCOLATES

APPLE PIE DONUT HOLES

MAKES 32 DONUT HOLES
Hands-on 40 min.
Total 1 hour, 25 min.

Don't wait for fall to roll around before whipping up these orchard-inspired gems.

1 (16.3-oz.) can refrigerated jumbo buttermilk biscuits
Vegetable oil
1 cup canned apple pie filling
Thick Vanilla Icing (p. 35)

Red food coloring paste
Red sanding sugar
32 ($\frac{1}{2}$-inch) pieces green sour candy straws
32 green gumdrops

1. Separate biscuits into individual rounds, and cut into quarters. Roll each quarter into a ball. Pour oil to depth of 2 inches into a Dutch oven; heat to 375°.

2. Fry balls, in batches, 30 seconds on each side or until golden. Drain on paper towels. Cool completely.

3. Process pie filling in a food processor until the texture of applesauce. Insert a round metal tip no. 5 into a large decorating bag; fill with pureed pie filling. Insert tip into each donut hole, and fill with a small amount of pie filling.

4. Prepare Thick Vanilla Icing. Tint icing with desired amount of food coloring paste to resemble the color of an apple. Dip donut holes in icing, letting excess drip back into bowl. Place dipped donut holes on a wire rack set over a baking sheet. Sprinkle with red sanding sugar. Let stand 30 minutes or until set. Insert 1 sour candy straw piece into each donut hole to resemble a stem.

5. Flatten gumdrops with a rolling pin; cut into leaf shapes with a small paring knife. Attach 1 gumdrop leaf to each stem.

NOTE: We tested with Sour Punch Apple Straws.

HOT TIP

Prepare the icing using apple cider instead of milk for even more apple flavor.

Homemade cookies-and-cream icing is the surprise inside these decadent donut holes. Add a few candles and serve them at a birthday party for an easy pick-up dessert buffet.

Chocolate Cake Donuts (p. 15) or 48 store-bought cake donut holes

½ recipe Cream Cheese Frosting (p. 35)

20 cream-filled chocolate sandwich cookies, divided

½ recipe Thick Vanilla Icing (p. 35)

Wax paper

1. Prepare Chocolate Cake Donuts, cutting dough into 48 donut holes using a 1½-inch round cutter and re-rolling dough once. Cool completely. (Do not dust with powdered sugar.)

2. Prepare ½ recipe Cream Cheese Frosting. Process 6 cookies in a food processor until finely ground; stir into frosting.

3. Insert round metal tip no. 5 into a large decorating bag; fill with frosting. Insert tip into side of each donut hole; pipe frosting into center of each donut hole.

4. Coarsely crush remaining 14 cookies.

5. Prepare ½ recipe Thick Vanilla Icing. Spread icing on tops of donut holes, allowing glaze to drip down sides; sprinkle icing with crushed cookies. Place on wax paper, and let stand until set.

COOKIES & CREAM DONUT HOLES

MAKES 48 DONUT HOLES
Hands-on 1 hour, 15 min.
Total 2 hours, 45 min.

DONUT

Which came first—the donut ring or the donut hole? They arrived at the same time in the early 1800s, when bakers realized that a donut would cook more evenly with a hole in the center!

TRIVIA

MICE DONUT HOLES

**MAKES 36 DONUT HOLES
Hands-on 1 hour, 15 min.
Total 3 hours, 25 min.**

Even though real mice are generally gray or brown, they are quite adorable in a purple hue. You might prefer pink or even light blue! Feel free to tint them any shade you like.

FLIP IT

Gather the kids and make these cute little edible mice for your next Halloween party or animal-themed birthday party.

Fried Cake Donuts (p. 12) or 36 store-bought cake donut holes

Thick Vanilla Icing (p. 35)
Purple food coloring paste
Parchment paper
108 mini-morsels
36 (2-inch) pieces
        licorice rope
72 sliced almonds

1. Prepare Fried Cake Donuts, cutting dough into 48 donut holes using a 1½-inch round cutter and re-rolling dough once. Cool completely. (Do not dust with powdered sugar.) Set aside 12 donut holes for another use.

2. Prepare Thick Vanilla Icing. Tint icing purple using desired amount of purple food coloring paste. Dip donut holes in icing, allowing excess to drip back into bowl. Place dipped donut holes on a wire rack set over a baking sheet lined with parchment paper. Let stand 10 minutes or until almost set.

3. Working with 1 donut hole at a time, adhere 2 mini-morsels for eyes and 1 mini-morsel for nose to donut hole. Make a small hole in back side of donut hole using a wooden pick. Insert 1 licorice piece for tail. Press pointed ends of 2 almond slices into top of donut hole for ears. Let stand 30 minutes or until set.

STARS & STRIPES DONUT POPS

MAKES 40 POPS • HANDS-ON 1 HOUR • TOTAL 1 HOUR, 30 MIN.

1 (12-oz.) can refrigerated
buttermilk biscuits

Vegetable oil

½ cup seedless strawberry jam

Thick Vanilla Icing (p. 35)

½ tsp. almond extract

Blue food coloring paste

Red and white star-shaped candy
sprinkles

Colorful paper straws or lollipop
sticks

1. Separate biscuits into individual rounds. Cut biscuits into quarters; roll quarters into balls. Pour oil to depth of 2 inches into a Dutch oven; heat to 375°.

2. Fry donut holes, in batches, 30 seconds on each side or until golden. Drain on paper towels.

3. Spoon strawberry jam into a pastry bag fitted with a no. 7 plain round tip. Insert tip into each donut hole; pipe a small amount of jam into center of donut holes.

4. Prepare Thick Vanilla Icing; stir in almond extract. Tint icing with blue food coloring paste. Dip donut holes in blue icing, letting excess drip back into bowl. Place dipped donut holes on a wire rack set over a baking sheet. Immediately sprinkle donut holes with candy sprinkles. Let stand 30 minutes or until set. Insert straws or lollipop sticks into donut holes.

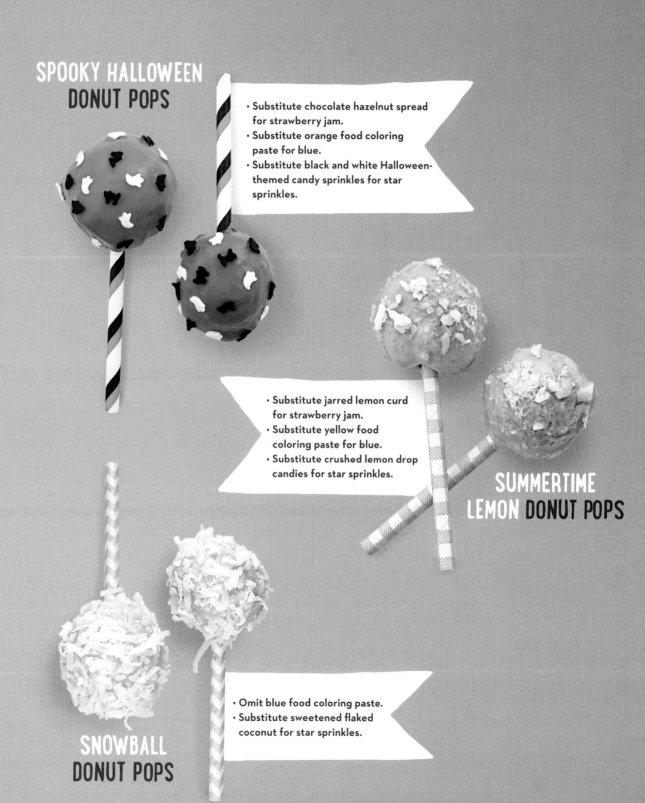

SPOOKY HALLOWEEN DONUT POPS

- Substitute chocolate hazelnut spread for strawberry jam.
- Substitute orange food coloring paste for blue.
- Substitute black and white Halloween-themed candy sprinkles for star sprinkles.

- Substitute jarred lemon curd for strawberry jam.
- Substitute yellow food coloring paste for blue.
- Substitute crushed lemon drop candies for star sprinkles.

SUMMERTIME LEMON DONUT POPS

- Omit blue food coloring paste.
- Substitute sweetened flaked coconut for star sprinkles.

SNOWBALL DONUT POPS

BUMBLEBEE DONUT HOLES

MAKES 15 DONUT HOLES
Hands-on 1 hour, 15 min.
Total 2 hours, 45 min.

HOT TIP

Check out the Donut Beehive on p. 130! If you're feeling ambitious, make both recipes, and use toothpicks to attach Bumblebee Donut Holes to the hive.

½ recipe Fried Cake Donuts (p. 12) or 15 store-bought cake donut holes

½ recipe Thick Vanilla Icing (p. 35)

Lemon yellow food coloring paste

Parchment paper

1 (0.67-oz.) tube black decorating gel

15 white candy wafers, cut in half

30 candy eyes

Black pull-apart string licorice, cut into ½-inch pieces

1. Prepare Fried Cake Donuts, cutting dough into 24 donut holes using a 1½-inch round cutter and re-rolling dough once. Cool completely. (Do not dust with powdered sugar.) Set aside 9 donut holes for another use.

2. Prepare ½ recipe Thick Vanilla Icing. Tint icing with yellow food coloring paste until a medium yellow color. Dip donut holes in icing, letting excess drip back into bowl; place on a wire rack set over a sheet of parchment paper. Let stand 30 minutes or until icing is set.

3. Working with 1 donut hole at a time, make 4 stripes on iced donut hole using black decorating gel to resemble a bumblebee's abdomen. Adhere 1 candy wafer half to each side with additional glaze to resemble wings. Attach 2 candy eyes to front of "bees." Insert 2 licorice pieces into donut hole to resemble antennae. Let donut holes stand 10 minutes or until attachments are firmly secured.

These crisp donut holes filled with marshmallow crème and dipped in a rainbow of colors are sure to be a hit at your next birthday party or school event.

RAINBOW DONUT HOLES

1 (16.3-oz.) can refrigerated jumbo buttermilk biscuits
Vegetable oil
¼ cup butter, softened
¾ cup powdered sugar
1 cup marshmallow crème
Thick Vanilla Icing (p. 35)
Red, yellow, green, blue, orange, and purple food coloring paste
Red, yellow, green, blue, orange, and purple sparkling sugar

MAKES 32 DONUT HOLES
Hands-on 35 min.
Total 1 hour, 15 min.

1. Separate biscuits into individual rounds, and cut into quarters. Roll each quarter into a ball. Pour oil to depth of 2 inches into a Dutch oven; heat to 375°.

2. Fry balls, in batches, 30 seconds on each side or until golden. Drain on paper towels. Cool completely.

3. Beat butter at medium speed with an electric mixer until creamy. Gradually add powdered sugar, beating well. Add marshmallow crème, beating until smooth. Insert a round metal tip no. 5 into a large decorating bag; fill with marshmallow crème mixture. Insert tip into each donut hole, and fill with marshmallow crème mixture.

4. Prepare Thick Vanilla Icing. Place about 6 Tbsp. icing in each of 6 bowls. Tint icing in each bowl a different color using desired amounts of red, yellow, green, blue, orange, and purple food coloring paste.

5. Working with 1 color of icing at a time, dip 5 to 6 donut holes in icing; sprinkle with corresponding color of sparkling sugar, and place on a wire rack on a baking sheet. Let stand until set.

HOT TIP

Arrange these donuts on a platter in a semicircle like a rainbow for a smart serving idea. Or display them on a flat white plate to resemble a painter's palette, as shown in the picture.

SALTED CARAMEL-CHOCOLATE DONUT POPS

MAKES 24 POPS
Hands-on 1 hour, 30 min.
Total 2 hours, 30 min.

½ recipe Raised Donuts (p. 18) or 24 store-bought yeast donut holes

½ cup thick caramel sauce

1 (6-inch) wooden skewer

1½ cups bittersweet chocolate chips

2 tsp. shortening

24 lollipop sticks

1 (18- x 16-inch) foam craft block

1 Tbsp. coarse sea salt

1. Prepare Raised Donuts, cutting dough into 24 donut holes using a 1½-inch round cutter. Cool completely. (Do not dust with powdered sugar.)

2. Spoon caramel sauce into a zip-top plastic freezer bag; seal bag. Snip 1 corner of bag to make a ¼-inch hole. Make a small hole in the side of each donut hole using a 6-inch wooden skewer. Squirt caramel sauce into each donut hole. (Do not overfill.)

3. Place chocolate chips and shortening in a small microwave-safe bowl. Microwave at HIGH 1 to 2 minutes or until melted and smooth, stirring every 30 seconds.

4. Dip the tip of 1 lollipop stick into melted chocolate; insert chocolate end of stick into hole where caramel was piped. Seal hole with additional melted chocolate. Place on a baking sheet. Repeat procedure with remaining sticks, melted chocolate, and remaining donut holes. Chill 15 minutes or until chocolate is set and donut holes are cold.

5. If necessary, microwave chocolate at HIGH 30 seconds or until pourable. Working with one pop at a time, remove from refrigerator and dip in melted chocolate, letting excess drip back into bowl. Stand donut pops upright by their sticks in foam block. Immediately sprinkle with sea salt. Let stand until chocolate is set.

FUZZY CHICKADEE DONUT HOLES

These whimsical chick donuts will get ooos and ahhs at your next springtime party. Place them in an egg carton for a cute serving idea.

Fried Cake Donuts (p. 12) or 36 store-bought cake donut holes

3 cups sweetened flaked
  coconut
Lemon yellow food
  coloring paste
Thick Vanilla Icing (p. 35)

72 mini-morsels
36 orange candy-coated
  sunflower seeds
36 pressed-sugar cake-
  decorating flowers

1. Prepare Fried Cake Donuts, cutting dough into 48 donut holes using a 1½-inch round cutter and re-rolling dough once. Cool completely. (Do not dust with powdered sugar.) Set aside 12 donut holes for another use.

2. Combine coconut and ⅛ tsp. yellow food coloring paste in a large zip-top plastic freezer bag. Seal bag and shake vigorously, mashing and mixing until coconut is evenly tinted yellow; place coconut in a medium bowl, and set aside.

3. Prepare Thick Vanilla Icing. Tint icing with yellow food coloring paste. Dip donuts completely in icing, allowing excess to drip back into bowl. Roll iced donuts in yellow coconut to cover.

4. Working with 1 donut hole at a time, place 2 mini-morsels at top of donut hole for eyes. Place 1 sunflower seed in center of face for beak. Place 1 sugar flower on top of donut.

MAKES 36 DONUT HOLES
Hands-on 1 hour, 15 min.
Total 2 hours, 45 min.

DONUT

Canada has the highest number of donut shops per capita in the whole world!

TRIVIA

BIRTHDAY CAKE DONUT HOLES

MAKES 48 DONUT HOLES
Hands-on 45 min.
Total 1 hour, 45 min.

Feel free to substitute your favorite flavor of ready-to-spread frosting in this recipe. You can even tint it any color to match the party decorations!

FLIP IT

With a coating of frosting and sprinkles inside and out, these donut holes are ideal for any party—especially birthdays!

Baked Donuts (p. 16) or 12 store-bought cake donut holes

Vegetable cooking spray
¼ cup rainbow candy sprinkles
2 (16-oz.) containers vanilla ready-to-spread frosting
¼ cup candy sprinkles in desired color

1. Preheat oven to 400°. Lightly grease both sides of 2 (12-cavity) cake ball pans with cooking spray. Prepare Baked Donuts batter (though step 2), stirring ¼ cup rainbow candy sprinkles into batter. Spoon batter into prepared pans, and assemble according to manufacturer's instructions.

2. Bake at 400° for 8 minutes or until light golden. Cool in pans on wire racks 2 minutes. Carefully remove donut holes from pans using an offset spatula. Transfer to a wire rack, and cool completely. Wash pans, lightly spray with cooking spray, and repeat filling, assembling, baking, and cooling with remaining batter.

3. Place frosting in a microwave-safe bowl. Microwave at HIGH 25 seconds or until pourable. Dip donut holes in melted frosting. Sprinkle evenly with ¼ cup sprinkles in desired color. Let stand until set.

Get glitzy with these sparkling and glittering pops made from store-bought donuts. Party prep couldn't be easier!

Baked Donuts (p. 16) or 12 store-bought cake donut holes

2 cups white candy melts

12 lollipop sticks

½ cup pink rock candy pieces

½ cup edible gold glitter

1 (18- x 16-inch) foam craft block photo

1. Prepare Baked Donuts. Cool completely. (Do not dust with powdered sugar.) Place candy melts in a medium microwave-safe bowl. Microwave at HIGH 1 minute or until melted and smooth, stirring every 15 seconds. Dip tips of lollipop sticks in melted candy; insert into bottoms of donut holes no more than halfway inside donut holes.

2. Place rock candy in a zip-top plastic freezer bag; crush into tiny pieces with a meat mallet or rolling pin. Reheat melted candy, if necessary. Working with 1 pop at a time, dip entire pop in melted candy, allowing excess to drip back into bowl. Immediately sprinkle with crushed rock candy and edible glitter. Place opposite end of stick into foam block. Let pops stand 5 minutes or until set.

GLAM DONUT POPS

MAKES 12 POPS
Hands-on 20 min.
Total 25 min.

DONUT

The size of the average donut hole is $4/5$ inch in diameter.

TRIVIA

KITTY CAT DONUT POPS

MAKES 12 POPS
Hands-on 55 min.
Total 1 hour, 25 min.

HOT TIP

Rice vermicelli noodles are the perfect squiggly edible sticks to use as whiskers for these kitties; however, you can use raw angel hair pasta in a pinch.

12 store-bought cake donut holes

2 cups orange candy melts
1 Tbsp. shortening
12 paper lollipop sticks
Parchment paper
1 (18- x 16-inch) foam craft block
24 orange candy-coated sunflower seeds
24 small white confetti candy sprinkles
12 pink heart-shaped candy sprinkles
72 (1-inch) pieces raw rice vermicelli noodles
½ cup black candy melts

1. Place orange candy melts and shortening in a small microwave-safe bowl. Microwave at MEDIUM (50% power) 2 to 3 minutes or until melted, stirring every 30 seconds.

2. Dip tips of lollipop sticks in melted candy; insert into bottoms of donut holes no more than halfway inside donut holes. Place on a parchment paper-lined baking sheet; chill 15 minutes.

3. Reheat melted candy, if necessary. Working with 1 pop at at time, dip entire pop in melted candy, allowing excess to drip back into bowl. Place opposite end of stick into foam block. Immediately attach 2 sunflower seeds for ears, 2 white candy sprinkles for eyes, and 1 heart-shaped candy sprinkle for nose. Insert 3 pieces rice vermicelli pieces on each side of nose for whiskers. Let stand 15 minutes or until set.

4. Place black candy melts in a small microwave-safe bowl; microwave at MEDIUM (50% power) 1 to 1½ minutes or until melted, stirring every 30 seconds. Insert plain round metal tip no. 3 into a large decorating bag; fill with black melted candy. Pipe mouth underneath nose. Pipe 1 black dot onto center of each white confetti candy sprinkle eye for pupils.

Frying cruller dough creates a delectable donut hole that's light and airy like a cream puff.

French Crullers (p. 28)

Vegetable oil

½ cup lemon curd

¾ cup whipping cream

½ cup plus 2 Tbsp. powdered sugar, divided

2 to 3 tsp. fresh lemon juice (1 lemon)

Yellow food coloring paste

1. Prepare French Cruller dough, following steps 2 and 3 of the recipe.

2. Pour oil to depth of 3 inches into a Dutch oven; heat to 375°. Using a 1¼-inch cookie scoop, drop dough, in batches of 8 scoops, into hot oil; fry 6 minutes, turning occasionally, or until puffed and deep golden brown. Drain on paper towels. Cool completely.

3. Place lemon curd in a medium bowl. Beat whipping cream and 2 Tbsp. powdered sugar at high speed with an electric mixer until stiff peaks form. Stir one-quarter of whipped cream into lemon curd; gently fold in remaining whipped cream. Cover and chill while preparing glaze.

4. Whisk together remaining ½ cup powdered sugar and lemon juice in a small bowl until drizzling consistency. Tint glaze with desired amount of yellow food coloring paste.

5. Insert an open star metal tip no. 21 into a large decorating bag; fill with whipped cream filling. Insert tip into side of each donut hole, and squeeze filling into center (do not overfill). Drizzle holes with glaze.

LEMON CRULLER DONUT HOLES

MAKES 28 DONUT HOLES
Hands-on 1 hour, 45 min.
Total 2 hours, 15 min.

HOT TIP

Using an open star tip makes it easier to pierce these donut holes, which are sturdier than donuts made with other types of dough. Serve assembled donut holes within 2 hours for best results.

CHOCOLATE & FRUIT DONUT KABOBS

MAKES 12 KABOBS • HANDS-ON 20 MIN. • TOTAL 55 MIN.

24 store-bought raised donut holes

12 (6-inch) wooden skewers

12 fresh strawberries, halved

½ fresh pineapple, peeled, cored, and cut into 12 (1-inch) pieces

2 (4-oz.) bittersweet chocolate baking bars, chopped

⅔ cup heavy cream

2 Tbsp. butter

1. Soak wooden skewers in water at least 30 minutes.

2. Preheat grill to 350° to 400° (medium-high) heat. Alternately thread 2 donut holes, 2 strawberry halves, and 1 pineapple piece onto each skewer. Grill, covered with grill lid, 1 to 2 minutes on each side or until grill marks appear.

3. Place chocolate in a medium bowl. Place cream and butter in a microwave-safe 2-cup glass measuring cup. Microwave at HIGH 1 to 1½ minutes or until boiling. Pour over chocolate. Let stand 5 minutes. Stir until smooth. Drizzle chocolate sauce over kabobs.

TROPICAL DONUT KABOBS

- Substitute 12 slices fresh kiwi, halved, and 12 pieces fresh banana for strawberries.
- Thread onto skewers.
- Sprinkle kabobs with toasted coconut.

S'MORE DONUT KABOBS

- Omit pineapple and strawberries.
- Thread 2 regular-sized marshmallows alternately with donut holes (24 marshmallows total) onto each skewer.
- Sprinkle with chopped graham crackers.

- Substitute 12 fresh blackberries and 24 fresh blueberries for pineapple.
- Thread 1 blackberry and 2 blueberries onto each skewer.
- Top or serve with sweetened whipped topping.

BERRIES 'N' CREAM DONUT KABOBS

ALL-STAR DONUT HOLES

GOOOOOO DONUTS! *Cheer on your favorite team with these champion donuts. They're sure to turn anyone into a good sport!*

3 dozen store-bought cake donut holes

Thick Vanilla Icing (p. 35)
Orange food coloring paste
Parchment paper
1 (4.25-oz.) tube black
    decorating icing
1 (4.25-oz.) tube red
    decorating icing

MAKES 36 DONUT HOLES
Hands-on 55 min.
Total 1 hour, 25 min.

1. Prepare Thick Vanilla Icing. Spoon 1¼ cups icing into a separate bowl; tint with desired amount of food coloring paste. (Do not tint remaining icing.) Dip 18 donut holes in orange icing, allowing excess to drip back into bowl. Place dipped donut holes on a wire rack set on a baking sheet lined with parchment paper. Repeat procedure with remaining 18 donut holes and white icing. Let stand 30 minutes or until set.

2. Pipe black decorating icing on orange donut holes to resemble basketballs. Pipe red decorating icing on white donut holes to resemble baseballs.

NOTE: We tested with Betty Crocker Decorating Icings.

Change up the food coloring and designs to represent tennis, soccer, golf, or any other sport you choose.

FLIP IT

DONUT
MASTERPIECES

The only thing better than a donut is lots of
donuts! Stack them up; add some glaze, whipped
cream, or frosting; and top with sprinkles
for an applause-worthy party treat.

HOW TO BUILD
A DONUT CAKE!

A donut cake is a spectacular treat for any party,
and it requires no baking or frying!

Start with a pedestal or plate, a variety of donuts with or without glaze (36 donuts to be exact), and 3 to 4 long wooden picks.

Arrage 7 donuts in a circle with 1 donut in the center. If desired, make each layer a different flavor of donut.

Build a second layer of donuts using 6 donuts to make a circle with 1 donut in the center.

Build a third layer of donuts using 6 donuts to make a circle and 1 donut in the center. Insert wooden picks to stabilize cake.

Repeat step 4 using 7 donuts, this time pushing donuts down onto picks, allowing them to pierce donuts all the way through.

Repeat step 5 using 7 donuts. Cut off any visible portion of picks. Top cake with icing, glaze, or frosting, and fresh fruit or candy.

BIRTHDAY DONUT MINI CAKES

MAKES 4 SERVINGS
Hands-on 1 hour
Total 2 hours, 25 min.

These mini donut cakes are a fun and easy alternative to traditional cakes for children's birthday parties.

Raised Donuts (p. 18) or 12 store-bought yeast donuts

½ recipe Thick Vanilla Icing (p. 35)

Pink food coloring paste

Lime-green candy sprinkles

2 cups thawed frozen whipped topping

Birthday candles

1. Prepare Raised Donuts. Cool completely. (Do not dust with powdered sugar.)

2. Prepare ½ recipe Thick Vanilla Icing. Tint with desired amount of pink food coloring paste, stirring until blended.

3. Frost tops of donuts with icing. Sprinkle with candy sprinkles. Let stand until set (about 10 minutes).

4. Assemble each mini cake: Place 1 frosted donut on a platter. Lightly frost the bottom of a second frosted donut, and place on top of first donut. Repeat procedure with a third frosted donut to form a stack.

5. Insert metal star tip into a large decorating bag; fill with whipped topping. Pipe whipped topping on top of donut stacks, and insert candles.

DONUT

In the U.S., some people lucked out with a pretty sweet name: Donut and Doughnut are real last names!

TRIVIA

NEAPOLITAN DONUT STACKS

MAKES 12 STACKS
Hands-on 25 min.
Total 25 min.

> 12 store-bought chocolate cake donuts

> 24 store-bought cake donuts

1½ cups butter, softened, divided

7 cups powdered sugar, divided

4 oz. semisweet chocolate, melted

1 Tbsp. milk

½ tsp. vanilla extract

⅔ cup finely chopped fresh strawberries

Chocolate sprinkles

Multicolored sprinkles

12 whole fresh strawberries

1. Beat ½ cup butter at medium speed with an electric mixer until creamy; gradually add 2 cups powdered sugar, beating until smooth. Add melted chocolate, beating at low speed. Add milk and vanilla, beating until blended.

2. Beat remaining 1 cup butter at medium speed with an electric mixer until creamy; gradually add remaining 5 cups powdered sugar alternately with strawberries, beating at low speed until blended and smooth. (If frosting is too thin, add additional powdered sugar; if too thick, add additional finely chopped strawberries.)

3. Spread chocolate frosting over tops of chocolate cake donuts; sprinkle with chocolate sprinkles. Spread strawberry frosting over tops of cake donuts; sprinkle with multicolored sprinkles.

4. Layer 1 strawberry-frosted cake donut, 1 chocolate-frosted chocolate cake donut, and 1 strawberry-frosted cake donut on a serving plate. Repeat procedure with remaining donuts, creating 12 stacks. Add a whole fresh strawberry on top of each stack. Cut stacks in half when ready to serve.

Create a Neapolitan Donut Cake by arranging these donut stacks as a cake. Look on p. 104 for How to Build a Donut Cake!

FLIP IT

BANANA CREAM PIE DONUT STACKS

MAKES 6 STACKS
Hands-on 15 min.
Total 15 min.

Echoing the flavors of banana cream pie, this sweet treat features bananas and cream nestled between layers of Boston cream donuts. Buy the "custard-filled" donuts instead of the "cream-filled" donuts if you're looking for true banana cream pie flavor.

12 store-bought Boston cream donuts with chocolate glaze

1¼ cups whipping cream
½ tsp. vanilla extract

2½ Tbsp. powdered sugar
3 medium-size bananas

1. Beat whipping cream and vanilla until foamy; gradually add powdered sugar, beating until soft peaks form.

2. Slice bananas.

3. Arrange 7 banana slices on top of 1 donut; repeat with remaining 5 donuts. Top each donut with ¼ cup whipped cream. Place another donut on top of whipped cream. Dollop remaining whipped cream on tops of donuts, and top with remaining banana slices. Serve immediately.

DONUT

The first written record of the "doughnut" is in an 1809 publication, *A History of New York*, written by Washington Irving.

TRIVIA

The donut holes resemble ice-cream scoops in this iconic ice-cream treat complete with split bananas and a cherry on top!

MINI BANANA SPLIT DONUT SUNDAES

2 dozen store-bought cake donut holes

Thick Vanilla Icing (p. 35)

Pink gel food coloring paste

Brown gel food coloring paste

8 large bananas, cut in half lengthwise

½ cup chocolate syrup

1 (8.5-oz.) can refrigerated instant whipped cream

Multicolored candy sprinkles

24 maraschino cherries with stems

1. Prepare Thick Vanilla Icing; divide into 3 bowls. Tint 1 bowl of icing with desired amount of pink food coloring, stirring until blended. Tint a second bowl of icing with desired amount of brown food coloring, stirring until blended. Do not tint remaining bowl of icing.

2. Dip 8 donut holes, 1 at a time, in pink icing, allowing excess to drip back into bowl. Let donut holes stand on a wire rack until set (about 3 minutes). Repeat procedure with 8 donut holes and brown icing and remaining 8 donut holes and white icing.

3. Place 2 banana halves in each of 8 small oblong dishes. Top banana halves in each dish with 1 donut hole of each color. Top each sundae with 1 Tbsp. chocolate syrup. Decorate sundaes with whipped cream. Sprinkle each sundae with sprinkles. Top each sundae with 3 cherries.

MAKES 8 SUNDAES
Hands-on 30 min.
Total 30 min.

PIÑATA DONUT CAKES

MAKES 4 SERVINGS
Hands-on 15 min.
Total 15 min.

Not only are store-bought donuts the perfect shortcut for homemade cake layers, they also come with a hole in the center that's perfect for a surprise candy filling!

12 store-bought cake donuts

1½ cups butter, softened

10 cups powdered sugar

1 cup finely chopped fresh strawberries

1 cup candy-coated chocolate pieces

Birthday candles (optional)

1. Beat softened butter at medium speed with an electric mixer until fluffy. Gradually add powdered sugar and chopped strawberries, beating at low speed until creamy.

2. Place 1 donut on a serving platter. Spread top of donut with strawberry frosting. (Do not allow frosting to fill donut hole.) Place a second donut on top of frosting. Spread frosting on top of second donut. Repeat procedure, stacking and spreading frosting on a third donut.

3. Pour ¼ cup candy pieces into center of donut stack. Firmly tamp down candies to fill donut holes. Repeat procedure with remaining donuts, frosting, and candy to create 4 donut cakes.

4. Spread remaining frosting on sides of donut cakes. Insert candles, if desired.

NOTE: We tested with M&M's.

A dowel will help you create straight, secure stacks of donuts, as pictured on the cover!

2 recipes Donut Machine Donuts (p. 20)

Thick Vanilla Icing (p. 35)

Electric-purple food coloring paste

Electric-blue food coloring paste

Electric-green food coloring paste

Lemon-yellow food coloring paste

Electric-orange food coloring paste

Light pink food coloring paste

Electric-pink food coloring paste

Rainbow candy sprinkles

1 (½-inch-diameter) wooden dowel (optional)

1. Prepare Donut Machine Donuts batter twice. (Do not double the recipe.) Fill cavities in a preheated mini donut machine according to recipe. Bake donuts according to manufacturer's instructions. Cool completely. (Do not dip donuts in chocolate glaze.)

2. Place about ⅓ cup Thick Vanilla Icing in each of 7 small bowls. Tint icing in each bowl with desired amount of a different color of food coloring paste.

3. Working with 1 color at a time (keep remaining bowls of icing covered with a damp towel to prevent drying out), spoon each color of icing over 5 donuts. Immediately sprinkle with candy sprinkles. Let stand 15 minutes or until set.

4. Place bright pink glazed donuts on a serving platter. If desired, hold dowel upright in center of each bright pink donut as you continue to stack 1 donut of each color on top of bright pink donuts, creating 5 stacks with colors in the following order: bright pink, pink, orange, yellow, green, blue, and purple. (Transfer dowel to another stack once each stack is complete.)

RAINBOW MINI DONUT STACKS

MAKES 12 STACKS
Hands-on 35 min.
Total 50 min.

You can create rainbow stacks of larger donuts by using Fried Cake Donuts (p. 12), Raised Donuts (p. 18), or store-bought unglazed cake or yeast donuts.

FLIP IT

CARAMEL CORN DONUT STACK

MAKES 8 SERVINGS
Hands-on 30 min.
Total 1 hour, 40 min.

Super-Quick Donut Holes (p. 23)

Vegetable cooking spray
1 (3.5-oz.) bag popped plain microwave popcorn
1 (3.5-oz.) bag honey-roasted almond slices
1 cup butter
2 cups firmly packed light brown sugar
½ cup sorghum syrup
1½ tsp. table salt
1 tsp. baking soda
½ tsp. almond extract
1½ cups candy-coated chocolate-covered peanuts

1. Preheat oven to 250°. Lightly coat a large bowl and a 15- x 10-inch jelly-roll pan with cooking spray. Combine popcorn and almonds in prepared bowl.

2. Melt butter in a large heavy saucepan over medium heat; stir in brown sugar and next 2 ingredients. Bring to a boil. Boil, without stirring, 4 minutes or until a candy thermometer registers 240°. Remove from heat; stir in baking soda and almond extract. Pour 1½ cups caramel over popcorn mixture, stirring to coat; reserve remaining caramel for later use. Transfer popcorn mixture to prepared pan, spreading into a thin layer. Bake at 250° for 1 hour, stirring every 15 minutes. Cool in pan on a wire rack 10 minutes. (Mixture will become crisp as it cools.)

3. Prepare Super-Quick Donut Holes, omitting cinnamon and sugar; keep warm.

4. Drizzle ½ cup reserved caramel onto a platter, reheating, if necessary. Stack donut holes in a pyramid shape on top of caramel. Drizzle ½ cup caramel over donut pyramid. Combine 5 cups caramel corn mixture and candy-coated peanuts; sprinkle over pyramid, pressing lightly to adhere. Reserve remaining caramel corn mixture for another use. Drizzle remaining ½ cup caramel over pyramid.

DONUT WREATH

This sweet wreath is perfect for a baby shower or birthday, but you can customize it for any occasion or to reflect the changing seasons.

Fried Cake Donuts (holes only) (p. 12) or 36 store-bought donut holes

Thick Vanilla Icing (p. 35)

Pink food coloring paste

Parchment paper

Pink sanding sugar or
   pink and white candy
   sprinkles

4 oz. store-bought pink
   rolled fondant

Powdered sugar

MAKES 18 SERVINGS
Hands-on 1 hour, 15 min.
Total 2 hours, 45 min.

1. Prepare Fried Cake Donuts, cutting dough into 48 donut holes using a 1½-inch round cutter and re-rolling dough once. Cool completely. (Do not dust with powdered sugar.) Set aside 12 donut holes for another use.

2. Prepare Thick Vanilla Icing. Divide icing in half, placing each half in a separate bowl. Tint half of icing light pink; tint remaining half of icing medium pink. Dip 16 donut holes in light pink icing, allowing excess to drip back into bowl. Place on a wire rack over parchment paper; immediately sprinkle with sanding sugar or candy sprinkles. Repeat procedure with remaining 16 donut holes and bright pink icing. Let stand 30 minutes or until set.

3. Arrange donut holes in a wreath shape on a platter. Roll out fondant to ⅛-inch thickness on a work surface lightly dusted with powdered sugar. Cut into 1-inch strips; shape strips into a decorative bow. Place bow on top of wreath.

HOT TIP

You can find fondant at crafts stores or online. To prevent it from drying out, wrap any remaining fondant in plastic wrap, and place in a plastic bag.

DONUT KING CAKE

MAKES 24 SERVINGS
Hands-on 1 hour, 15 min.
Total 2 hours, 30 min.

Surprise your valentine
with a donut heart.
Arrange donuts into
a heart instead of a
ring and sprinkle with
red or pink candies
and sprinkles.

FLIP IT

To assemble this Donut King Cake in a jiffy for your next Mardi Gras celebration, purchase unglazed yeast donut holes at the bakery.

Raised Donuts (p. 18) or 60 store-bought yeast donut holes

Thick Vanilla Icing (p. 35)   Yellow sparkling sugar
Purple sparkling sugar   Green sparkling sugar

1. Prepare Raised Donuts, cutting dough into donut holes with a 1-inch cutter. Cool completely. (Do not dust with powdered sugar.)

2. Arrange 60 donut holes on a large platter, stacking as necessary to form a wreath. Reserve remaining 12 donut holes for another use.

3. Prepare Thick Vanilla Icing. Pour icing over wreath, letting some drip down sides. Sprinkle sparkling sugars over icing in alternating bands of purple, yellow, and green. Let stand 20 minutes or until icing is set.

DONUT HOLE
BANANA PUDDING

MAKES 6 TO 10 SERVINGS • HANDS-ON 1 HOUR, 55 MIN. • TOTAL 5 HOURS, 10 MIN.

**Raised Donuts (p. 18) or
60 store-bought yeast donut holes**

1 cup sugar

3 Tbsp. cornstarch

¼ tsp. table salt

4 cups milk

4 egg yolks

2 tsp. vanilla extract

6 medium-size ripe bananas, sliced

1 cup whipping cream, whipped

1. Prepare Raised Donuts, cutting dough into donut holes with a 1-inch cutter. Cool completely. (Do not dust with powdered sugar.)

2. Whisk together sugar, cornstarch, and salt in a heavy saucepan. Gradually whisk in milk and egg yolks. Cook over medium heat, whisking constantly, 13 minutes or until thickened and smooth. Remove from heat; stir in vanilla. Pour mixture into a bowl. Place heavy-duty plastic wrap directly on warm custard (to prevent a film from forming); chill. (Mixture will thicken as it cools.)

3. Layer half of donut holes on bottom and around sides of 6 (5-inch) ramekins or dishes or 1 (3-qt.) bowl. Top with half of banana slices. Spoon half of pudding over banana slices. Repeat layers once. Spread or pipe whipped cream over top of pudding. Cover and chill 2 hours.

CHOCOLATE-STRAWBERRY DONUT TRIFLE

- Whisk ¼ cup cocoa powder into sugar-cornstarch mixture.
- Substitute 6 cups sliced fresh strawberries for bananas.
- Drizzle ⅓ cup warmed hot fudge sauce over each layer of pudding and on top of dessert (1 cup total).

PEANUT BUTTER-BANANA DONUT PUDDING

- Stir ½ cup creamy peanut butter into hot cooked pudding.
- Sprinkle ½ cup chopped chocolate peanut butter cups onto each layer of pudding and on top of dessert (1½ cups total).

COCONUT-BANANA DONUT PUDDING

- Substitute 4 cups coconut milk for milk in pudding.
- Sprinkle ½ cup toasted coconut over each layer of bananas and on top of dessert (1½ cups total).

FRESH BERRY DONUT CHARLOTTE

MAKES 14 SERVINGS
Hands-on 25 min.
Total 25 min.

DONUT

The Dutch are traditionally recognized as bringing donuts to the U.S. around 1847. They were called "olykoek" or "oily cake."

TRIVIA

14 store-bought French cruller donuts

2 tsp. unflavored gelatin
2 Tbsp. cold water
2 cups heavy whipping cream
¼ cup powdered sugar
1 cup small strawberries, hulled
½ cup fresh blackberries
½ cup fresh raspberries

1. Sprinkle gelatin over 2 Tbsp. cold water in a small saucepan. Let stand 1 minute. Cook over low heat, stirring until gelatin dissolves. Remove from heat; cool 5 minutes.

2. Beat whipping cream at high speed with a heavy-duty electric stand mixer, using a whisk attachment, until foamy. With mixer on, add gelatin mixture to cream. Gradually add powdered sugar, beating until stiff peaks form. Insert a large metal star tip into a decorating bag; fill with whipped cream mixture.

3. Place 1 donut in center of a large round serving platter. Pipe whipped cream onto donut to cover. Place another donut on top of whipped cream. Arrange remaining 12 donuts, upright on their sides, around center stack, forming a 10-inch circle.

4. Pipe whipped cream vertically between outer donuts. Pipe small rosettes of whipped cream on top of donut ring. Pile strawberries, blackberries, and raspberries in center of donut ring.

NOTE: We tested with Dunkin' Donuts French Crullers.

OMBRE DONUT CAKE

To create a showstopping birthday cake, dip donuts in bright pink, orange, and purple hues. Stack the dipped donuts shortly before serving, and top with candles.

Fried Cake Donuts (p. 12) or 35 store-bought cake donuts

Thick Vanilla Icing (p. 35)

Electric-purple food coloring paste

Magenta food coloring paste

Electric-pink food coloring paste

Peach food coloring paste

Orange food coloring paste

Assorted purple, pink, and orange sprinkles, sugars, or nonpareils

1. Prepare Fried Cake Donuts dough 3 times. (Do not triple the recipe.) Cool completely. (Do not dust with powdered sugar.) Reserve donut holes for another use.

2. Prepare Thick Vanilla Icing recipe 3 times. Place about 1½ cups icing in each of 5 bowls. Tint icing in each bowl a different color using food coloring pastes.

3. Working with 1 color at a time (keep remaining bowls of icing covered with a damp towel to prevent drying out), dip 7 donuts completely in icing. Immediately sprinkle with corresponding colors of sprinkles or sugars as desired. Place donuts on a wire rack set over a baking sheet. Let donuts stand 1 hour or until icing is set.

4. Arrange 7 purple donuts in a circular layer on a serving platter, placing 1 donut in center surrounded by 6 donuts, sides touching. Top with 1 layer each of magenta donuts, pink donuts, peach donuts, and orange donuts.

MAKES 20 SERVINGS
Hands-on 1 hour, 30 min.
Total 4 hours

Switch up the colors on this cake to match your favorite sports team or to match any holiday celebration.

FLIP IT

DONUT BEEHIVE

MAKES 12 SERVINGS
Hands-on 20 min.
Total 20 min.

Your guests will be buzzing with delight when they lay eyes on this sweet bee-utiful donut cake, made simple using store-bought donuts.

17 store-bought unglazed cake donuts

Thick Vanilla Icing
(p. 35)

Lemon-yellow food
coloring paste

1 store-bought unglazed
chocolate cake donut

Wooden picks

Candy bees

1. Stack 5 cake donuts in center of a serving platter. Arrange 5 donuts around center stack. Cut 7 cake donuts in half vertically, creating 14 half moons. Arrange 5 half moons, cut sides inward, on top of the 5-donut layer; repeat layer once. (Alternate half moons in each layer from the layer below as in the different courses of a brick wall.) Arrange remaining 4 half moons, cut sides inward, on top of the last layer.

2. Prepare Thick Vanilla Icing using 1/2 cup milk. Tint icing with desired amount of yellow food coloring paste. Drizzle icing over hive.

3. Cut 1 inch from bottom of chocolate cake donut to create a horseshoe shape; attach donut horseshoe, cut side down, to bottom layer of hive for a door using wooden picks. Arrange candy bees onto hive.

GERMAN CHOCOLATE DONUT CAKE

18 store-bought chocolate cake donuts

18 store-bought chocolate cake donut holes

1½ cups sugar

1 (12-oz.) can evaporated milk

4 large egg yolks

¾ cup butter, cut into small pieces

2 tsp. vanilla extract

2 cups chopped toasted pecans

1 (7-oz.) package sweetened flaked coconut

½ recipe Classic Chocolate Glaze (p. 32)

Additional sweetened flaked coconut

1. Whisk together sugar, milk, and egg yolks in a 3-qt. saucepan. Add butter, and bring to a simmer over medium heat, whisking constantly. Cook, whisking constantly, 10 minutes or until thickened. Remove from heat; stir in vanilla and next 2 ingredients. Place plastic wrap directly onto warm custard (to prevent a film from forming), and cool completely.

2. Arrange 6 donuts in a circle on a serving platter; spread with one-third of coconut-pecan filling. Repeat layers twice, ending with filling. Arrange 18 donut holes on top.

3. Prepare ½ recipe Classic Chocolate Glaze. Drizzle top with glaze, and sprinkle with additional sweetened flaked coconut.

MAKES 18 SERVINGS
Hands-on 40 min.
Total 1 hour, 40 min.

Substitute old-fashioned donuts and donut holes in place of the chocolate and omit the chocolate glaze for an Italian Donut Cream Cake.

FLIP IT

DONUT MIX-UP

What do you get when you cross a donut with another wondrous dessert? A "Wonderdonut!" Check out all these amazing treats you get when you combine a donut with just about anything else you can imagine!

DOFFLES

MAKES 12 SERVINGS
Hands-on 25 min.
Total 1 hour, 15 min.

"Doffles" are made from a sweet yeast donut dough that is cooked in a waffle iron instead of fried. Topped with a purple maple glaze, these are the perfect hybrid of donut and waffle. We prefer them studded with blueberries. For more options to try see p. 138-139.

1 cup warm milk
   (100° to 110°)

¼ cup granulated sugar

1 (¼-oz.) envelope active
   dry yeast

2 cups all-purpose flour

⅓ cup butter, melted

1 tsp. table salt

1 large egg, lightly beaten

1 cup fresh blueberries
   (optional)

2 cups powdered sugar

1 cup maple syrup

Purple food coloring paste
   (optional)

1. Stir together first 3 ingredients in a large glass bowl; let stand 5 minutes.

2. Stir in flour and next 3 ingredients until blended. Cover with a damp kitchen towel, and let stand 45 minutes. If desired, stir in 1 cup fresh blueberries.

3. Cook in a preheated oiled Belgian waffle iron until golden.

4. Combine powdered sugar and maple syrup in a small bowl. Tint glaze purple, if desired. Dip warm waffles in glaze; place on a wire rack. Serve warm, or cool completely on rack until glaze is set.

DONUT

The largest statue in the U.S. is located in California at Randy's Donuts, and it measures 22 feet in diameter.

TRIVIA

CRAZY FOR
DOFFLES

These donuts crossed with a waffle are just BEGGING for some fun flavor combinations! Just follow the steps below using the basic Doffles recipe on p. 136 to create endless Doffle possibiities.

 +  + +

MIX
BATTER

Make 1 recipe Doffle batter (p. 136), omitting blueberries and glaze.

STIR IN
FLAVOR

Stir fresh fruit, chocolate chips, nuts, or coconut into batter. Cook according to recipe.

DRIZZLE
ICING

Drizzle cooked Doffles with maple syrup, icing, glaze, or even ice cream toppings such as caramel.

SPRINKLE
TOPPINGS!

Sprinkle Doffles with more fresh fruit, candy, nuts, or sprinkles!

= MANY DELICIOUS COMBINATIONS

Create your own Doffle match-ups, or try one of our genius combinations. →

BIRTHDAY CAKE DOFFLES

- Stir ½ cup multicolored sprinkles into Doffle batter.
- Drizzle with Strawberry Icing (p. 35).
- Sprinkle with additional multicolored sprinkles.

RASPBERRY DOFFLES

- Gently stir 1 cup raspberries into Doffle batter.
- Drizzle cooked Doffles with Vanilla Glaze (p. 32).
- Sprinkle with additional raspberries.

TOASTED COCONUT DOFFLES

- Stir ¾ cup sweetened flaked coconut into Doffle batter.
- Drizzle cooked Doffles with Vanilla Glaze (p. 32).
- Sprinkle with toasted coconut flakes.

CHOCOLATE-PECAN DOFFLES

- Stir ½ cup chopped pecans into Doffle batter.
- Drizzle cooked Doffles with Classic Chocolate Glaze (p. 32).
- Sprinkle Doffles with additional chopped pecans.

LEMON-POPPY SEED DOFFLES

- Stir 2 Tbsp. poppy seeds and 1 Tbsp. lemon zest into Doffle batter.
- Drizzle cooked Doffles with yellow-tinted Thick Vanilla Icing (page 35).
- Sprinkle with additional poppy seeds.

CARAMEL-WALNUT DOFFLES

- Stir ½ cup chopped walnuts into Doffle batter.
- Drizzle cooked Doffles with caramel ice cream topping.
- Sprinkle Doffles with additional chopped walnuts.

BANANA DOFFLES

- Stir ¾ cup mashed bananas into Doffle batter.
- Mix together Vanilla Glaze (p. 32) and 2 Tbsp. dark brown sugar; drizzle over cooked Doffles.
- Sprinkle Doffles with sliced fresh bananas.

PEANUT BUTTER CUP DOFFLES

- Stir ½ cup mini morsels into Doffle batter.
- Drizzle cooked Doffles with Peanut Butter Frosting (p. 35).
- Sprinkle Doffles with additional mini morsels.

CRANBERRY-ORANGE DOFFLES

- Stir ½ cup dried cranberries into Doffle batter.
- Drizzle cooked Doffles with orange-tinted Vanilla Glaze (p. 32).
- Sprinkle Doffles with orange zest and additional dried cranberries.

Wake up to donuts AND flapjacks! Stack them high or enjoy one at a time, but don't forget the butter and syrup.

1 recipe Baked Donut batter (p. 12)

Sifted powdered sugar

1 cup fresh blueberries

1 cup sliced strawberries

½ cup maple syrup

Butter, optional

1. Prepare Baked Donut batter.

2. Pour about ¼ cup batter for each flapjack onto a hot, lightly greased griddle or large nonstick skillet. Cook pancakes over medium heat 2 to 3 minutes or until tops are covered with bubbles and edges look dry and cooked; turn and cook other side.

3. Place 3 flapjacks on each of 4 plates. Dust with powdered sugar, and top with berries. Drizzle with syrup; serve with butter, if desired.

DONUT FLAPJACKS WITH BERRIES

MAKES 4 SERVINGS
Hands-on 26 min.
Total 36 min.

For Chocolate Chip Donut Flapjacks, omit berries and stir ½ cup mini morsels into batter. Cook flapjacks as directed.

FLIP IT

CHERRY-FILLED DOISSANTS

MAKES 16 SERVINGS
Hands-on 30 min.
Total 1 hour

Refrigerated crescent roll dough forms the base of these donut-croissant hybrids. Stuff them with your favorite preserves, and drizzle with a pretty ruby red glaze.

2 (8-oz.) cans refrigerated crescent rolls	Vegetable oil
1 large egg, lightly beaten	Vanilla Glaze (p. 32)
⅓ cup cherry preserves	¼ tsp. almond extract
	Red food coloring paste

1. Unroll 1 can of dough at a time, leaving remaining can of dough in refrigerator. Separate dough into quarters, using horizontal and vertical perforations. Firmly pinch diagonal perforations to seal. Cut each dough rectangle crosswise into 3½-inch squares. Brush edges of squares with egg. Spoon 1 tsp. cherry preserves into center of each square; fold 1 corner of dough over filling to opposite corner to create triangles, pressing edges together with a fork to seal. Freeze 30 minutes or until firm.

2. Pour oil to depth of 3 inches into a Dutch oven; heat to 375°. Fry triangles, in batches, 1 minute on each side or until golden. Drain on paper towels.

3. Prepare Vanilla Glaze, adding almond extract. Tint glaze with desired amount of red food coloring paste. Spoon frosting into a zip-top plastic freezer bag. Snip 1 corner of bag to make a small hole. Squirt a zigzag drizzle of glaze over donuts.

LEMON-BLUEBERRY
DUFFINS

MAKES 12 SERVINGS • HANDS-ON 24 MIN. • TOTAL 45 MIN.

Baked Donuts (p. 16)

Vegetable cooking spray

2 tsp. lemon zest, divided

½ cup sugar

¼ cup butter, melted

¾ cup blueberry preserves

1. Preheat oven to 400°. Lightly grease a 12-cup muffin pan with cooking spray.

2. Prepare Baked Donuts through step 2, adding 1 tsp. lemon zest to batter. Divide batter evenly among muffin cups.

3. Bake at 400° for 16 minutes or until golden brown and a wooden pick inserted in center comes out clean. Cool 5 minutes; remove from pans.

4. Meanwhile, combine sugar and remaining 1 tsp. lemon zest in a small bowl. Brush warm Duffins with melted butter; roll in lemon sugar.

5. Spoon blueberry preserves into a pastry bag fitted with a no. 5 plain tip. Insert tip into bottom or side of each Duffin, and squirt about 1 Tbsp. blueberry preserves into center of each.

RASPBERRY-LIME DUFFINS

- Substitute lime zest for lemon zest.
- Substitute raspberry preserves for blueberry preserves.

- Substitute 2 tsp. ground cinnamon for lemon zest.
- Stir ½ cup chopped toasted pecans into donut batter.
- Substitute canned dulce de leche for blueberry preserves.

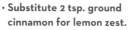

CARAMEL-NUT DUFFINS

CRANBERRY-ORANGE DUFFINS

- Substitute orange zest for lemon zest.
- Substitute cranberry sauce or preserves for blueberry preserves.

HAZELNUT DONUCCINO

MAKES 4 SERVINGS
Hands-on 5 min.
Total 5 min.

Serve this breakfast-inspired beverage with a straw. For an even sweeter mocha flavor, use chocolate-covered cake donuts.

2 store-bought cake donuts, divided

2 cups coffee ice cream, softened

²/₃ cup milk

¼ cup hazelnut spread

2 Tbsp. hazelnut-flavored coffee liqueur

Whipped cream

2 Tbsp. chocolate sauce

¼ cup toasted chopped hazelnuts

4 (6-inch) wooden skewers

1. Process 1 donut (cut into 1-inch pieces), ice cream, milk, hazelnut spread, and liqueur in a blender until smooth, stopping to scrape down sides as needed. Pour into 4 glasses. Top each shake with a dollop of whipped cream. Drizzle chocolate sauce over whipped cream; sprinkle with hazelnuts.

2. Cut remaining donut into 1-inch pieces. Thread pieces onto skewers. Add 1 skewer to each glass.

NOTE: We tested with Nutella and Kalúha Hazelnut Liqueur.

Not only is this one of the easiest donut recipes around, but it also deliciously combines two breakfast favorites—donuts and cinnamon rolls. Don't forget the glaze!

CINNAMON ROLLNUTS

MAKES 16 SERVINGS
Hands-on 17 min.
Total 17 min.

2 (12.4-oz.) cans
    refrigerated cinnamon
    roll dough

Vegetable oil

1. Separate roll dough into 16 individual rolls. Cut holes in center of rolls using a 1-inch cutter or the removable center of a donut cutter. Reserve holes. Set icing aside.

2. Pour oil to depth of 2 inches into a Dutch oven; heat to 350°. Fry donuts and donut holes, 4 each at a time, 1 to 1½ minutes on each side or until golden brown. Drain on paper towels.

3. Transfer icing to a 1-qt. zip-top plastic freezer bag. Snip 1 corner of bag to make a small hole. Squirt a zigzag drizzle over donuts.

DONUT

Female Salvation Army workers became known as "Doughnut Girls" on the front lines of World War I, where they would cook and distribute donuts to the soldiers.

TRIVIA

PUFFED DONUTS

MAKES 9 SERVINGS
Hands-on 18 min.
Total 18 min.

Prepared puff pastry makes for an exceptionally flaky "donut" that gets even crispier and flakier when fried.

Vegetable oil

1 (17.3-oz.) box frozen puff pastry, thawed

1 large egg, lightly beaten

Vanilla Glaze (p. 32)

Nonpareils

1. Pour oil to depth of 3 inches into a large Dutch oven; heat over medium-high heat to 375°.

2. Unfold each dough sheet onto a lightly floured surface; roll to an 11-inch square. Brush 1 sheet with egg; top with second sheet, pressing to seal. Cut 9 circles from dough using a 3½-inch donut cutter.

3. Fry donuts and holes, in batches, in hot oil 3 to 4 minutes or until golden. Drain on a paper-towel lined baking sheet. Drizzle with Vanilla Glaze, and sprinkle with nonpareils.

Cut into strips, these donuts resemble a plate of French fries with a side of ketchup, but taste like sweet donuts with glaze!

Raised Donuts (p. 18)

Vegetable oil   Red food coloring paste

Vanilla Glaze (p. 32)

1. Prepare Raised Donuts through step 2.

2. Roll dough into a 9- x 8-inch rectangle (about 1/8 inch thick). Cut rectangle crosswise into thirds, creating 3 (8- x 3-inch) rectangles. Cut each rectangle crosswise into 16 (1/2-inch-wide) strips. (You should have 48 strips.)

3. Pour oil to depth of 2 inches into a Dutch oven; heat to 350°. Fry strips, in batches, 30 seconds on each side or until golden. Drain on paper towels.

4. Prepare Vanilla Glaze. Tint glaze red with food coloring paste. Drizzle red glaze over fries, or serve alongside.

FRENCH FRIED DONUTS

MAKES 8 SERVINGS
Hands-on 30 min.
Total 1 hour, 30 min.

HOT TIP

For ease in cutting dough into strips, use a pizza cutter or pastry wheel.

PEANUT BUTTER DONUT S'MORES

MAKES 6 SERVINGS
Hands-on 20 min.
Total 20 min.

This is a great way to liven up day-old store-bought or homemade yeast donuts. They are delicious on their own as a sweet, crispy snack, but even better when sandwiched with marshmallows, peanut butter, and chocolate!

6 store-bought glazed raised donuts

½ cup creamy peanut butter

2½ cups miniature marshmallows

3 (1.55-oz.) milk chocolate candy bars, broken in half

1. Cut donuts in half horizontally using a serrated knife (do not separate halves). Cook 3 whole donuts in a preheated panini press 2 minutes or until deep golden brown. Remove to a wire rack to cool completely. Repeat with remaining 3 donuts. Carefully separate donut halves, using a serrated knife to re-cut if necessary.

2. Preheat broiler with oven rack 4 inches from heat. Place donut halves, cut sides up, on an aluminum foil-lined baking sheet. Spread evenly with peanut butter; sprinkle with marshmallows.

3. Broil 30 seconds or until marshmallows are lightly browned. Remove from oven; top 6 donut halves with half of 1 chocolate bar. Top with remaining 6 donut halves, marshmallow side down. Serve immediately.

When fresh strawberries are in season, there's nothing quite like Strawberry Shortcake-except for Strawberry Donut Shortcakes, of course! Be sure to use fresh whipped cream for an authentic flavor.

STRAWBERRY DONUT SHORTCAKES

MAKES 6 SERVINGS
Hands-on 12 min.
Total 42 min.

6 store-bought cake donuts

4 cups sliced fresh strawberries

½ cup granulated sugar

2 tsp. chopped fresh mint

1 tsp. lemon zest

1 cup heavy cream

½ tsp. vanilla extract

2 Tbsp. powdered sugar

1. Combine first 4 ingredients in a medium bowl. Let stand 30 minutes, stirring occasionally.

2. Combine cream and vanilla; beat until foamy. Gradually add powdered sugar, beating until soft peaks form.

3. Cut donuts in half horizontally. Place 1 donut bottom on each of 6 plates. Top evenly with strawberry mixture and whipped cream. Cover with donut tops.

Give these desserts a "chocolate-covered strawberry" spin by replacing the cake donuts with chocolate cake donuts.

FLIP IT

EASY DONUT SUNDAES

MAKES 6 SERVINGS
Hands-on 9 min.
Total 9 min.

Whip up these impressive treats in no time with store-bought ice cream, toppings, and donuts. Serve them for a kids' slumber party or movie night.

6 store-bought chocolate-glazed raised donuts

¾ cup chocolate ice cream

¾ cup strawberry ice cream

¾ cup vanilla ice cream

6 Tbsp. hot fudge topping, warmed

6 Tbsp. chopped walnuts

2 Tbsp. multicolored sprinkles

6 Tbsp. frozen whipped topping, thawed

6 maraschino cherries with stems

1. Place 1 donut on each of 6 serving plates. Scoop 2 Tbsp. chocolate ice cream, 2 Tbsp. strawberry ice cream, and 2 Tbsp. vanilla ice cream onto each donut.

2. Top each sundae with 1 Tbsp. hot fudge topping, 1 Tbsp. chopped walnuts, 1 tsp. sprinkles, 1 Tbsp. whipped topping, and 1 maraschino cherry. Serve immediately.

BANANA-CARAMEL DONUT PUDDINGS

MAKES 6 SERVINGS
Hands-on 20 min.
Total 45 min.

6 store-bought glazed raised donuts

Vegetable cooking spray

2 bananas, thinly sliced

2½ cups whipping cream, divided

1 cup creamy European cookie spread (such as Lotus Biscoff), divided

2 Tbsp. light brown sugar

2 large eggs

1¼ cups granulated sugar, divided

¼ cup light corn syrup

Garnish: vanilla ice cream

1. Preheat oven to 375°. Lightly grease 6 (8-oz.) ramekins with cooking spray. Tear donuts, 1 at a time, into pieces. Place the pieces of 1 donut into each prepared ramekin. Top each with one-sixth of banana slices.

2. Heat 1¾ cups whipping cream in a medium saucepan over medium heat. Whisk in ½ cup cookie spread until blended. Whisk brown sugar, eggs, and ½ cup granulated sugar in a medium bowl until blended. Gradually whisk in cream mixture. Pour custard mixture evenly into ramekins. Place ramekins on a large rimmed baking sheet. Bake at 375° for 25 minutes or until set, golden brown, and slightly puffed.

3. Meanwhile, bring corn syrup, ¼ cup water, and remaining ¾ cup granulated sugar to a boil in a medium saucepan over high heat. (Do not stir.) Boil, swirling occasionally after sugar begins to change color, 7 minutes or until dark amber. (Watch carefully.) Remove from heat. Carefully whisk in remaining ¾ cup cream (mixture will bubble and spatter). Whisk constantly until bubbling stops. Whisk in remaining ½ cup cookie spread until smooth. Spoon about 2 Tbsp. warm caramel sauce over puddings.

HOT TIP

Store any remaining caramel sauce in an airtight container in the refrigerator for up to 2 weeks. Reheat on the stovetop over low heat, or microwave at MEDIUM (50% power).

BERRIES & CREAM DONUT NAPOLEONS

MAKES 8 SERVINGS
Hands-on 12 min.
Total 12 min.

These cute and colorful donut stacks with luscious lemon cream and fresh berries will brighten up your next luncheon.

1 dozen store-bought glazed raised donuts, halved horizontally

1 pt. fresh strawberries, quartered

1 pt. fresh blueberries

2 (6-oz.) containers fresh raspberries

2 Tbsp. granulated sugar

1 (8-oz.) container mascarpone cheese, softened

1 tsp. lemon zest

1 cup powdered sugar, divided

2 Tbsp. fresh lemon juice (1 lemon), divided

1 cup whipping cream, whipped

1 cup seedless raspberry jam

1. Combine first 4 ingredients in a large bowl.

2. Whisk together mascarpone cheese, lemon zest, ½ cup powdered sugar, and 1 Tbsp. lemon juice until smooth. Fold in whipped cream. Insert large metal star tip into a large decorating bag; fill with cream mixture. Chill until ready to use.

3. Combine raspberry jam and remaining 1 Tbsp. lemon juice in a small saucepan; place over medium heat, and cook, stirring constantly, 1 minute or until jam melts. Keep warm.

4. Place 1 donut half, cut side up, on each of 8 plates. Pipe about ¼ cup cream mixture onto each donut half; top each with about ¼ cup fruit. Repeat layers once. Top each stack with 1 donut half, cut side down.

5. Drizzle napoleons with warm raspberry sauce. Dust with remaining ½ cup powdered sugar.

DONUT

No one knows who first thought of using hot oil to cook pastry, but one story traces back to colonial times when a cow kicked a pot of hot oil onto dough.

TRIVIA

CHOCOLATE CHIP DONUT COOKIES

MAKES 10 COOKIES • HANDS-ON 24 MIN. • TOTAL 2 HOURS, 48 MIN.

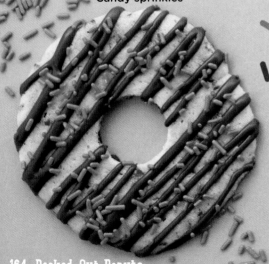

2 cups all-purpose flour

½ tsp. baking powder

¼ tsp. table salt

¾ cup butter, softened

1 cup sugar

1 large egg

2 Tbsp. milk

1 tsp. vanilla extract

¾ cup mini-morsels

Parchment paper

Classic Chocolate Glaze
(p. 32)

Candy sprinkles

This cookie dough is rolled, cut, and glazed to look like a donut. The cookies are softer and more cake-like than typical rolled sugar cookies but have that nutty sweetness characteristic of chocolate chip cookies.

1. Combine first 3 ingredients in a small bowl. Combine butter and sugar in a large bowl; beat at medium speed with an electric mixer until light and fluffy. Add egg, beating until blended. Add milk and vanilla, beating well. Gradually add flour mixture, beating on low speed until blended. Stir in mini-morsels. Shape dough into a flat disc; wrap in plastic wrap, and chill 2 hours.

2. Preheat oven to 350°. Place dough on a lightly floured surface, and roll to ¼-inch thickness. Cut dough with a 3½-inch donut cutter. Separate donut shapes from holes, and place both on baking sheets lined with parchment paper.

3. Bake at 350° for 12 minutes or until edges are lightly browned. Cool on baking sheets 2 minutes. Transfer to a cooling rack. Cool completely.

4. Prepare Chocolate Glaze. Immediately spread or drizzle glaze over cookies; sprinkle with candy sprinkles.

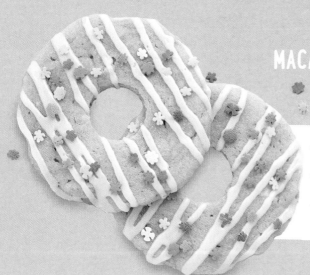

MACADAMIA–WHITE CHOCOLATE
DONUT COOKIES

- Substitute white chocolate morsels for mini-morsels.
- Add ½ cup chopped toasted macadamia nuts to dough.
- Substitute Vanilla Glaze (p. 32) for Classic Chocolate Glaze.

BIRTHDAY
DONUT COOKIES

- Substitute multicolored sprinkles for mini-morsels.
- Substitute Vanilla Glaze (p. 32) tinted pink or blue for Chocolate Glaze.

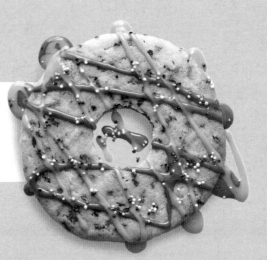

PEANUT BUTTER
DONUT COOKIES

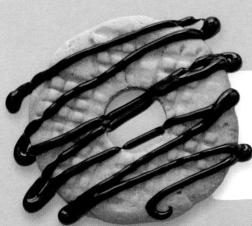

- Omit mini-morsels and sprinkles.
- Add ¾ cup crunchy peanut butter to butter-sugar mixture.
- Press fork tines into top of unbaked cookies for cross-hatch effect.

DONKEY BREAD

MAKES 8 TO 10 SERVINGS
Hands-on 25 min.
Total 1 hour, 55 min.

Raised Donuts (p. 18)

1 cup chopped pecans, toasted and divided

1 cup firmly packed light brown sugar

2 Tbsp. shortening

¾ cup butter

1 cup granulated sugar

Vanilla Glaze (p. 32)

1½ tsp. ground cinnamon

Purple food coloring gel

½ cup butter, melted

Confetti candy sprinkles

1. Prepare Raised Donut dough through step 2. Roll dough into an 8- x 6-inch rectangle (about 1 inch thick) on a floured surface. Cut dough into 48 (1-inch) squares. Roll each square into a ball.

2. Sprinkle ½ cup pecans in bottom of a greased (with shortening) 8-cup Bundt pan. Combine granulated sugar and cinnamon in a large zip-top plastic freezer bag.

3. Place ½ cup melted butter in a medium bowl. Working in batches, dip balls in melted butter, and place in sugar mixture. Seal bag; shake to coat. Place coated balls in prepared Bundt pan. Sprinkle with remaining ½ cup pecans. Cover and let rise in a warm place (85°), free from drafts, 45 minutes or until doubled in bulk.

4. Preheat oven to 350°. Place brown sugar and ¾ cup butter in a small saucepan. Cook, stirring with a whisk, over medium-high heat until butter melts and mixture comes to a boil. Boil, whisking constantly, 1 minute; pour over donut balls.

5. Bake at 350° for 40 minutes or until golden brown. Cool in pan on a wire rack 5 minutes. Invert onto a serving platter.

6. Tint Vanilla Glaze light purple with food coloring gel. Pour glaze over warm bread. Sprinkle confetti candy sprinkles over glaze.

GIANT DONUT CAKE

Cake mix makes this recipe quick and easy, but you can easily substitute your favorite yellow cake recipe. Look for a giant donut cake pan set online.

1 (15.25-oz.) package butter recipe yellow cake mix
1 cup milk
⅓ cup butter, softened
3 large eggs
Shortening
Flour
½ recipe Thick Vanilla Icing (p. 35)
1 (16 oz.) container ready-to-spread chocolate frosting
Teal food coloring paste
2 Tbsp. rainbow candy sprinkles

1. Preheat oven to 350°. Beat cake mix, milk, butter, and eggs at low speed with an electric mixer 30 seconds. Beat at medium speed 2 minutes.

2. Spoon batter into both sides of a greased (with shortening) and floured (8-inch) giant donut cake pan set.

3. Bake at 350° for 28 to 30 minutes or until a wooden pick inserted in center comes out clean. Cool in pans 10 minutes; remove from pans to a wire rack, and cool completely (about 1 hour).

4. Prepare ½ recipe Thick Vanilla icing; tint with desired amount of food coloring paste. Place 1 donut cake layer, rounded side down, on serving platter; spread with chocolate frosting. Top with second donut cake layer, rounded side up. Spoon teal icing over cake; sprinkle with candy sprinkles.

MAKES 12 SERVINGS
Hands-on 20 min.
Total 1 hour, 58 min.

DONUT

The largest donut ever made was an American-style jelly donut that weighed 1.7 tons and measured 16 feet tall and 16 feet wide.

TRIVIA

INDEX

Metric Equivalents

The recipes that appear in this cookbook use the standard U.S. method for measuring liquid and dry or solid ingredients (teaspoons, tablespoons, and cups). The information in the following charts is provided to help cooks outside the United States successfully use these recipes. All equivalents are approximate.

Metric Equivalents for Different Types of Ingredients

A standard cup measure of a dry or solid ingredient will vary in weight depending on the type of ingredient. A standard cup of liquid is the same volume for any type of liquid. Use the following chart when converting standard cup measures to grams (weight) or milliliters (volume).

Standard Cup	Fine Powder (ex. flour)	Grain (ex. rice)	Granular (ex. sugar)	Liquid Solids (ex. butter)	Liquid (ex. milk)
1	140 g	150 g	190 g	200 g	240 ml
3/4	105 g	113 g	143 g	150 g	180 ml
2/3	93 g	100 g	125 g	133 g	160 ml
1/2	70 g	75 g	95 g	100 g	120 ml
1/3	47 g	50 g	63 g	67 g	80 ml
1/4	35 g	38 g	48 g	50 g	60 ml
1/8	18 g	19 g	24 g	25 g	30 ml

Useful Equivalents for Dry Ingredients by Weight

(To convert ounces to grams, multiply the number of ounces by 30.)

1 oz	=	1/16 lb	=	30 g
4 oz	=	1/4 lb	=	120 g
8 oz	=	1/2 lb	=	240 g
12 oz	=	3/4 lb	=	360 g
16 oz	=	1 lb	=	480 g

Useful Equivalents for Length

(To convert inches to centimeters, multiply the number of inches by 2.5.)

1 in			=	2.5 cm		
6 in	=	1/2 ft	=	15 cm		
12 in	=	1 ft	=	30 cm		
36 in	=	3 ft	=	1 yd	90 cm	
40 in			=	100 cm	= 1 m	

Useful Equivalents for Liquid Ingredients by Volume

1/4 tsp				=	1 ml	
1/2 tsp				=	2 ml	
1 tsp				=	5 ml	
3 tsp	=	1 Tbsp		= 1/2 fl oz	=	15 ml
		2 Tbsp	= 1/8 cup	= 1 fl oz	=	30 ml
		4 Tbsp	= 1/4 cup	= 2 fl oz	=	60 ml
		5 1/3 Tbsp	= 1/3 cup	= 3 fl oz	=	80 ml
		8 Tbsp	= 1/2 cup	= 4 fl oz	=	120 ml
		10 2/3 Tbsp	= 2/3 cup	= 5 fl oz	=	160 ml
		12 Tbsp	= 3/4 cup	= 6 fl oz	=	180 ml
		16 Tbsp	= 1 cup	= 8 fl oz	=	240 ml
		1 pt	= 2 cups	= 16 fl oz	=	480 ml
		1 qt	= 4 cups	= 32 fl oz	=	960 ml
				33 fl oz	= 1000 ml	= 1 l

Useful Equivalents for Cooking/Oven Temperatures

	Fahrenheit	Celsius	Gas Mark
Freeze water	32° F	0° C	
Room temperature	68° F	20° C	
Boil water	212° F	100° C	
Bake	325° F	160° C	3
	350° F	180° C	4
	375° F	190° C	5
	400° F	200° C	6
	425° F	220° C	7
	450° F	230° C	8
Broil			Grill

©2015 Time Inc. Books

1271 Avenue of the Americas,
New York, NY 10020

ISBN-13: 978-0-8487-4443-4

ISBN-10: 0-8487-4443-8

Library of Congress Control
Number: 2015931553

Printed in the United States
of America

First Printing 2015

Cover recipe:
Rainbow Mini Donuts Stacks, p. 117

Oxmoor House

Creative Director: Felicity Keane
Art Director: Christopher Rhoads
Executive Photography Director: Iain Bagwell
Executive Food Director: Grace Parisi
Managing Editor: Elizabeth Tyler Austin
Assistant Managing Editor: Jeanne de Lathouder

Simply Sweet Decked-Out Donuts

Editor: Allison Cox Vasquez
Project Editor: Sarah Waller
Editorial Assistant: April Smitherman
Designer: Maribeth Jones
Assistant Test Kitchen Manager: Alyson Moreland Haynes
Recipe Developers and Testers: Stefanie Maloney,
    Callie Nash, Karen Rankin
Food Stylists: Nathan Carrabba, Victoria E. Cox,
    Margaret Monroe Dickey, Catherine Crowell Steele
Photo Editor: Kellie Lindsey
Senior Photographer: Hélène Dujardin
Senior Photo Stylists: Kay E. Clarke, Mindi Shapiro Levine
Associate Production Manager: Amy Mangus
Assistant Production Manager: Diane Rose Keener

Contributors

Interim Executive Editor: Katherine Cobbs
Recipe Editor: Julia Christopher
Copy Editors: Julie Bosche, Jaqueline Giovanelli
Proofreader: Rebecca Henderson
Indexer: Nanette Cardon
Food Stylist: Erica Hopper
Photographer: Becky Luigart-Stayner
Photo Stylists: Mary Clayton Carl, Melissa Crawford,
    Lydia DeGaris Pursell, Leslie Simpson
Fellows: Laura Arnold, Kylie Dazzo, Nicole Fisher,
    Loren Lorenzo, Anna Ramia, Caroline Smith,
    Amanda Widis

Time Inc. Books

Publisher: Margot Schupf
Vice President, Finance: Vandana Patel
Executive Director, Marketing Services: Carol Pittard
Executive Director, Business Development: Suzanne Albert
Executive Director, Marketing: Susan Hettleman
Assistant General Counsel: Simone Procas
Assistant Project Manager: Allyson Angle